A Hedonist's Guide to

Life

Edited by Fleur Britten

A Hedonist's Guide to Life

Managing director Tremayne Carew Pole
Marketing director Sara Townsend
Design Jason Morris
Sub-editor Janine Thomas
Publisher Filmer Ltd
Printers Printed in Italy by Printer Trento

Email life@hg2.com
Website www.hg2.com

First published in the United Kingdom in October 2007 by
Filmer Ltd
47 Filmer Road
London
SW6 7JJ

ISBN – 978-1-905428-20-5

The views and experiences of the writers herein are their own, and you follow their advice at your own risk.

Contents

▦ Play

▦ Trouble

▦ Clean(ish) Highs

Opposite: James Muldowney

Max Oppenheim/Getty Images

Dear Disgusted of Tunbridge Wells, Small-Minded of Small-Town America, curmudgeons the world over,

We've been expecting you – welcome to the party! Sorry if you're choking on your hot milk, we really are, but if we may be so bold, might we suggest that you've taken things a little too literally. We are not saying that the only road to pleasure is via wanton, filthy self-destruction, to be walked with legs akimbo while grabbing at drugs by the fistful. (Though if this were the case, we'd only be holding a mirror to what is the current age of hedonism).

We get that the pursuit of pleasure is not just about raging peak highs, but also plateaus of quiet contentment and the refreshing power of variety. The pleasure-peddlers within this guide do not comprise a unified voice. Instead, presented here is a pluralist take: less versus more, clean versus dirty. After all, hardcore hedonism takes up a lot of oxygen. Plus, there's taste to consider: one man's hedonism is another's hardship. We believe in the spirit of Whatever Works for You, be that simple pleasures, guilty pleasures, black pleasures, carnal pleasures, altruism, even religious ecstasy. There is room for all. It doesn't mean to say that we are for or against any of them, more that they are suggestions to help you find your pleasures and to understand others'.

For on the pages that follow is simply an anthology of possibilities, the thread of which is the very great importance of pleasure itself.

Another organising principle is honesty: brave, unguarded honesty. We are not afraid to admit it – sex, drugs and rampant drunkenness are, for some, a path to spiritual enlightenment. To get sky-high and unshackle our inhibitions is to enable a journey of self-discovery; travelling into the dusty corners of our higher consciousness is edifying and enriching. The enlightened hedonist knows that there is more out there.

And hedonism makes us happy. To be euphoric and on the edge is to kiss joy in flight. Everyone should be free to taste that. It's a necessity of life, because the world hurts. Tune into the latest bad news on teenage terrorists, homeless polar bears, wheelie-bin arson and skies falling in, and only the stoniest of souls are spared a nagging sense of nihilistic defeat. No wonder society is binge-drinking and binge-shagging in fuck-it escapism. While hedonism is no cure-all, it certainly eases the pain and exorcises our stress.

The final unifying spirit is humour. So, please, dear Disgusteds and Small-Mindeds, don't take it all too seriously. A Hedonist's Guide to Life is never going to become a school set text. Rather, its aim is to bring a little much-needed amusement into play. But then again, this gives you something to moan about. And moaning is your personal pleasure, isn't it? Perhaps it makes your blood pressure rise – like drugs, that's not very good for you – but then you get to ride the high of anger and the rush of self-righteousness. Don't worry – we understand! We all have our funny little ways, we're all sensation-seekers in one way or another, so let us be, and let us share our experiences with anybody who chooses to listen. Let them make up their own minds.

However, if you're really red with rage, please do write in. Really! We can publish all your tutting letters in a toilet book – and then that's another tidy little number ready for next Christmas, and you did all the work, leaving us free to play. We can party on the proceeds. What fun we will have.

Secretly, you are just a little bit curious about what joys lie on the other side, aren't you? For it is you, oh esteemed sensiblists of the world, that prove the purpose of this book – there really are people that need to be shown how to have fun. So come on, escape yourselves. Smoke a cigar! Throw a fancy-breast party! Dress like a drag queen! Live life, before it's too late. ❖

A Hedonist's Manifesto

Dearly beloved, we are gathered here today to get through This Thing Called Life...

We worship the unholy trinity of sex, drugs and rock'n'roll

We throw our knickers to the wind. If we're wearing any

We go where the wind blows us. (We leave our knickers just where they landed)

We live for the moment. We commit to the moment. Tomorrow is not a concern tonight

We like the night – sacred land of the Other Side. Hello darkness, my old friend

Sunrises are better than sunsets. Unless it's your second sunset without sleep

We take our full quota of statutory sick days. And "moving" days. And "bereavement" days. Know your rights!

If you don't ask, you don't get

We observe rules like a herd of Hindu cows (see "rule", read: suggestion)

We like life on the edge. From here you can see all the things you can't from the centre

We don't judge others' pleasures. We taste them for ourselves. We might just like them

We never say never

We make mistakes. We are "testing our boundaries"
No regrets, no guilt, no shame
Yes to peace, love and truth
We always travel with a hip flask
Give love, get love. Give drink, get drink
Personal happiness is paramount – yours, ours, theirs
We respect the virtues of risk, taboo, controversy, freewheeling and skinny-dipping
The world needs hedonists. Who wants to party with their accountant?

Chorus (all together now):

Be young, be foolish, be happy
You've got to fight. For the right. To party
Pump up the volume, pump up the volume, dance, dance
And if the elevator tries to bring you down, go crazy – punch a higher floor. Let's go crazy, let's get nuts, look for the purple banana, till they put us in the truck. Let's go!

You may now kiss life

Let's get naked! ❖

1

Food
and drink

" Food has replaced
sex in my life, now
I can't even get
into my own pants "

Anonymous

Opposite: Rockford

For the Love of Lunch

By Joseph Connolly

Joseph has penned 10 novels, the latest of which is Jack the Lad and Bloody Mary. His listed hobbies in Who's Who are lunching and loafing, which just about says all you need to know about the man (or want to)

YOU MAY HAVE HEARD the hideous rumour that the great days of lunch are a thing of the past. Remember? The aperitif stiffener, the white closely followed by the red, the three full courses (four if the restaurant runs to a decent cheese board), the coffee and chockies, maybe a liqueur, or else the third and injudicious bottle of claret. Something urgent must be done to save this endangered species. We must all eat lunch!

Proper lunch starts with good company (and just the two of you is always preferable to three, which is tricky: unless lifelong buds or even more, three-plus is just a meeting, with food). For all the joys that a great lunch has to offer, they fade and sour if your companion isn't into it, heart and soul. Your lunch mate must be similarly possessed of a keen appetite – for food, wine and wit. And a talent for truancy, since at least three hours is required. We can't have the sort of people who hope you won't mind if this is just a quick one because they've got to dash back for a meeting. Nor those who say, "Well, I'm not having a starter, but I insist that you do." And certainly not those who tell you that if a whole bottle is ordered, you'll be drinking nearly all of it yourself (a lie, anyway, particularly with women – the type who never order chips but always nick yours). Nor can you have anybody who is recovering from something, coming down with something, on the wagon, on the dole, off their food or off their heads. And we can do without vegetarians and people who are "intolerant" of perfectly innocuous things (such as food and drink, for Christ's sake). And preferably not someone you've not lunched with before (unless the express intention is to form a liaison, in which case lunch should idle along bibulously and segue seamlessly into dinner and beyond).

Then there is the business of the restaurant. Everyone will have their favourites: learn from this. Once you truly love a place, weld yourself to it, and it will love you back. Regularity is key: once the front of house and waiting staff know you by name, you will be able to select your table of preference; after a while, you can request it by phone; and after a further while, you will not have to – it is your table now. Essential, too, in a fashionable place (nothing wrong with fashionable, unless that's all it is), is the secret telephone number. There always is one, and if you are frequent, personable and regularly drop a socking fortune, it will be slipped unto you. First-name terms with the top-hatted doorman is a bonus (an initial tenner will generally secure this). However, never presume upon your relationship with a restaurant: always book, always remember to cancel. In return, you should never be refused a table (your table) and you should expect to be squeezed in somewhere if ever you turn up on spec.

Now, to lunch. Relax. Glass of champagne. Relax. Have a chat with the waiter about this and that, and even the menu – he should be friendly, seemingly pleased to see you (not too chummy, and never unctuous). There will be no problem catching his eye later on in the meal, because he remembers your policy of adding a bit of cash to the discretionary (ie mandatory) 12% service. But unless the staff are really tip-top, insist that your wine and water are left on the table and not five yards away (for everyone's sake). Decent sommeliers are there to help, not intimidate, and occasionally you ought to accept their recommendation (though always know its price). If a wine is off, say so. A proper establishment will not sniff or taste it, let alone argue – you will be offered an apology and a replacement. You might care to announce that it is your birthday: champagne will be forthcoming. It's as well not to have half-a-dozen birthdays a year, though (fair's fair, after all).

And now just look how the time has flown: laughter, good food, peerless service, too much wine and it's nearly 5pm. I really do love this place, don't you? We simply must come again soon.

Tomorrow suit you? ❖

A Table for One

By Dom Joly

Dom is a lonely comedian and traveller of the world

TRUE HAPPINESS TAKES total selfishness. Having a meal alone in a top restaurant ticks all my boxes – food, alcohol, being pampered, being selfish and listening in on everyone else's conversations. I'm an obsessive eavesdropper, which often causes problems when I'm out with my wife or friends as they accuse me of being rude and ignoring them. On my own, I'm free to do what I like.

It's not that I don't like the company of others for a good meal. It's just that sometimes I love the self-indulgence of the solo dining experience. It's a great way to take the temperature of a place – sitting back with a fantastic bottle of wine (all mine), people-watching, with a little spot of eavesdropping as a bonus. In Hanoi, I once overheard an Australian woman discussing how she was going to kill her husband. She went into quite some detail and her dopey girlfriend seemed to be doing very little to dissuade her. Back in London, at one of my favourite solo haunts – the bar of J Sheekey – I've listened to hopefuls try to bullshit film directors and blag £10m, and once overheard a distraught Sloane Ranger get the results of a biopsy (it was bad… very bad).

There's also a certain "fuck-you" element to eating on your own. With the fear of solitude being so prevalent in our society, dining alone can be very empowering when done voluntarily. It projects a feeling of confidence and independence that laughs in the face of that fear. When I was younger, I hated being on my own. I used to always try to fill my time, block out the "voices". It's only since turning 30 that I've learnt to enjoy it (come to think of it, maybe I was a schizophrenic and just didn't realise...? Who said that?).

Jonny Mendelsson

I always take a book, something quite highbrow that I can get my teeth into between succulent courses and other people's conversations. I'm writing this from Corsica, sitting in the port of Calvi, with George Orwell's Why I Write on the table in front of me. I can't wait to get stuck in, and my experience will definitely be enhanced by a tall glass or three of pastis and *une assiette* of freshly caught fish. Here I can pretend to be an intellectual, an artist, a bohemian or a deaf-and-dumb travelling juggler – whatever I want because nobody will bother to check the truth. It's pure escapism.

Without the incessant interruption of chatter from my own table, my ideas are free to take form. Columns, characters and jokes fly about during my solo meals. It's like 100 strangers pitching me free ideas that I can either accept or reject at will, without so much as a grimace or a thank you.

Then there's the complete control over my environment. Should I feel like it, I can eat and drink myself into a stupor without ever worrying about having to make witty or coherent conversation. Conversely, I can sit, eat and walk within half an hour and not feel the pressure to make every meal out some kind of special event.

> **❛ I can eat and drink myself into a stupor without ever worrying about having to make witty or coherent conversation ❜**

One of my favourite solo meals of all time was in California. I was in the gorgeous Redwood Room Bar of the Clift Hotel in San Francisco and I overheard a woman tell a friend about a great fish restaurant in Monterey. On a whim, I drove down there the next day and had an unbelievably wonderful meal for one – enormous, green-lipped mussels, saffron potatoes, creamed spinach and half a bottle of Gevrey-Chambertin, if I remember rightly. I was reading a brilliant book by Steve Martin called, rather appropriately, The Pleasure of My Company. It was a perfect day and I was back in Frisco in time to meet friends for the evening (it does happen occasionally, promise… Oh my God I'm now worried that you think I'm a lonely loser and I'm starting to have to justify myself…. I never worry like this in restaurants… I promise that I never stand up and shout, "I'm here on my own because I love it and choose to be, not because everyone hates me and I don't have any friends…" I really don't do that ever… I'm a hedonist… Be strong… Eat alone). ❖

How to Seduce... with Champagne
By Lucas Hollweg

Lucas is a journalist who has flirted with
food and drink from an indecently young age

THIS IS A MATTER about which I am approached for advice more
frequently than any other. It is a skill that is likely to be called into
service regularly throughout adult life – particularly among those of
good breeding – and it is doubtless for this reason that young men
experience such acute anxiety when their prowess is tested for the first
time. My counsel is always the same: a solid grounding in technique
will prevent even the most nervous of novices from appearing
inexperienced. I can think of no better teacher in this regard than the
late Earl of Orpington, who always approached his subject with lusty
passion. His memoir, Popping Corks: A Lifetime's Encounters with
Bubbly Friends, contains a useful 10-point plan, which should be the
constant companion of every young buck. I have taken the liberty of
reproducing his guidelines below.

Step 1: Chill for at least two hours beforehand – essential for enjoying
the experience to the full.
Step 2: Position yourself on a stout chair or sofa. Some men prefer to
stand, but in my view, this show-off tendency carries an unacceptable
risk of injury.
Step 3: Use your fingers to locate the closure around the neck and
quickly undo it. Don't worry if you find this a little fiddly; it remains
complicated, even after years of practice. Bear in mind, though, that
prolonged delay is likely to be frustrating and may ruin the moment.
Step 4: Peel off the top, taking care to control the pressure. It is all too
easy to take someone's eye out with a premature pop, especially if there
has been undue agitation beforehand.
Step 5: Grip firmly and turn, tilting to 45 degrees as you do so. You
should hear a gentle exhalation. Anything more is likely to leave you
with a nasty stain on the soft furnishings. You may wish to have a small

Mark Mainz/Getty Images

towel ready to deal with any unfortunate accidents.

Step 6: Insert thumb in bottom: by far the most elegant approach and will show that you are a man of experience. Grasping clumsily at the middle – or worse, the neck – will mark you out as a rank amateur.

Step 7: Take a nicely proportioned "coupe" in one hand and moisten as you see fit. Savour the moment. (A note on size: big ones are regarded as somewhat gauche. In my view, all have their merits, although I would concede that small ones feel nicer in the mouth.)

Step 8: Take in the colour. It's not uncommon to find anything from blushing pink to a rich gold. My personal preference has always been for the latter; the Italians, curiously, seem to favour a greenish tinge.

Step 9: Inhale deeply. What do you smell? A certain yeastiness is normal, but there may also be a slight whiff of apples, pears or even peaches. Depending on vintage, you might also expect to detect a hint of biscuit or perhaps brioche. The latter is more usual in the grand houses of France, and also in some of the more sophisticated Aussies and New Zealanders. Only you can know which of the above is most appealing. Personally, nothing arouses my interest like the lingering aroma of toast.

Step 10: Drink deep, or taste not the Pierian spring.

Having used the above strategy on countless occasions, I can say that the results have never been anything less than intoxicating. On which note, I have found that it works just as well as a guide to the enjoyment of champagne as to the modus operandi of seduction – worth bearing in mind if ever grappling with both at the same time.

In these circumstances, a little ostentatious spending goes a long way. Few women – or indeed men – can fail to notice a bottle of Krug or Dom Pérignon. And remember that vintage, though more expensive, is generally a more fulfilling experience, and in good years, even those houses whose usual blends leave one's stomach clamouring to exit via one's throat can produce a bubbly that is rich and rounded. I find this enables you to drink considerably more – seldom a bad thing.

A final note: be prepared to experiment with small houses. Not only are many of these a good deal cheaper than the grandes marques, but you may well turn up an idiosyncratic gem. Many is the time I have regaled a lover with my intimate knowledge of a Diebolt-Vallois, Larmandier-Bernier or Egly Ouriet.

Something to remember if ever your physical charms let you down. ❖

Eat Lobster in a War Zone

By Martin Deeson

Martin, a journalist and GQ columnist, has always thought that lobster was overrated, but found the three war zones he has been to surprisingly fun. But then again, he was a long way from the bullets

ONE OF THE most memorable people I have met in my journalistic career was Viktor Humanski, a Ukrainian ex-KGB man turned blood-diamond dealer who lived with three prostitutes in Freetown, Sierra Leone. Humanski came about as close to evil incarnate as I have ever witnessed. He did, however, always know where to get the best seafood, even as the rebel forces of the RUF surrounded Freetown, high on prescription drugs and ready to hack the limbs off anybody in their path.

> **❛I have experienced few feelings more intoxicating than stepping out of a Russian helicopter in Freetown with a notebook and a bunch of dollars in my pocket❜**

At times like this, even the most liberal representatives of the world's press, doctors of medical charities and dedicated NGO employees feel justified in eating lobster and drinking champagne as all around them descends into the heart of darkness. War does strange things to your head. It can make people euphoric, it can make the wife and polite society seem a long way from home, and it can make drinking malt whisky while those around you starve to death seem entirely necessary. It can also be a massive buzz – like being on the set of Apocalypse Now with an expense account. War zones are glamorous places if you are paid to visit them. I have experienced few feelings more intoxicating than stepping out of a Russian helicopter in Freetown with a notebook and a bunch of dollars in my pocket.

In the worst parts of the world, some people are having a very good

Toby Morison

time indeed. UN aid workers, arms dealers and internationally minded rock stars do not go to war zones to live like those who suffer – they go to do good, and therefore feel wholly justified in taking their metropolitan lifestyles with them. I once asked a very senior BBC reporter in Rwanda how it felt to eat his packed lunch (prepared by his £100-a-night hotel) in the middle of the world's largest refugee camp. "I just remind myself that I am there to report on the famine, not to take part in it," he replied. "And I have a bottle of Laphroaig and a couple of Cohibas back at the hotel to take my mind off it." As a man who has done inestimable amounts of good through his reporting – and seen more wars than almost any soldier – who can deny his need to preserve his sanity? If you do this year in, year out, then why the hell shouldn't you have the same standard of living as the people back home to whom you are reporting?

The fact is that very few people other than journalists, profiteers and NGO employees will ever see a war zone. And that's probably the best way to keep it. However, if you do ever find yourself in such a situation, the best way to enjoy shellfish while the shells fall is as follows:

1. Work for the UN

When I was in Sierra Leone, there were more white UN Land Cruisers in Freetown than there had been cars in the entire country before the war – and a huge number were sitting in ditches where they had been run off the road by drunken aid workers on the way back from bars.

2. Hang out with mercenaries

War is an increasingly privatised industry. And the £500-a-day, ex-SAS, Russian ex-Spetsnaz or American ex-Delta Force "security" employees will always find a way to enjoy drugs, sex, fine food and cold beer in even the most inhospitable environments.

3. *Cherchez l'hack*

Journos shun hardship as much as anybody with an expense account shuns an empty belly. Where two or three foreign correspondents are gathered together you will always find a bottle of Johnny Walker Black Label and 200 Marlboro Reds.

4. Stay close to those rich enough to have personal protection

Anybody with a bodyguard somewhere dangerous is not going to be living off club sandwiches back at the hotel. Arms and diamond dealers enjoy the best standard of life in the world's hellholes, but even those on the war tour – aid workers, fixers, mercenaries and journalists – tend to live in five-star hotels and dine on the finest food (unimaginable to the people in misery around them).

That is why men still make war – the spoils are good. And to live well in a war zone, all you need do is ensure that you are not making the news, you are just reporting on it, profiting from it or are a long way away from the danger.❖

The Wisdom and Folly of Whisky

By Joseph Connolly

Joseph has authored 10 novels, the latest of which is Jack the Lad and Bloody Mary. He was introduced to the stuff in the Highlands. This evolved into a sometimes stormy relationship that somehow endures

WHISKY, EH? Quite a minefield – though one that is admittedly a breathtaking delight to gingerly tiptoe one's meandering way through (the occasional misstep and resulting explosion being in every way a bit of a blast). Traditionally, one looks to the Scots for guidance – which can strike some as on a par with entrusting the finer points of fire safety to a cadre of recidivist arsonists – but at least the Scots are, if vertical, relatively united on the matter.

In the old days, before the global fascination with single malts took a stranglehold, there seemed to be only one whisky the Scots had any time for – Bell's, a serviceable brand that had never to be asked for by name in Scotland's pubs. And back then, there was no question of what to put in your Bell's – nothing else would do but yet another Bell's. A few of the more determined would have a Bell's or so as a chaser; others bypassed not just the niceties, but the agonising wait for the hammering effect, by pouring the Scotch straight into ale. This is called boozing.

But these days (they tell us), it is all about connoisseurship and nuance. A touch of Highland Spring water, it is said, will release the peaty or flowery bouquets, hitherto swirling away amid the oily gold. This is true of malts – particularly the ones that taste like a bonfire in a chemical lab (Laphroaig, most notably) – but go at the Bell's with water and you get watery whisky. Britain is nearly alone in not doing ice, though soda is making something of a comeback, partly due to the glamour of the siphon on the silver tray in those stylish, black-and-white films (the American ones, though, where someone such as Cary Grant deftly adds a perfectly judged whoosh to his poison, not the English ones, where a cackling Norman Wisdom joyously squirts the thing down a toff's trousers). And talking of America, it has always been regarded as far more sophisticated to drink scotch there, largely because it is imported, and is therefore more expensive than bourbon (Jack Daniel's having been hugely contributory to making the good old US of A just what it is today). But try suggesting to a bellicose Irishman that there might, you know, exist a Scotch whisky a tad superior to an Irish one such as Bushmills, and see what you get. In traction, actually, is what you'll get.

And it is the single malts that really rule. As recently as 30 years ago, Glenmorangie was virtually unknown outside Scotland. Now, in every decent bar in the world, you will find half-a-dozen variations (my favourite being Port Wood Finish – warm and pinkish, mellow and smooth, and if you do it right, it gets you drunk in rather a glorious manner: a roseate glow overcomes you and you can't stop smiling).

Which brings us to whisky-tasting – a grand thing to blag your way into (dress well, nod a lot), but do only bother with the very top-end whiskies in specialist dealers such as Milroy's in London, or Royal Mile Whiskies in Edinburgh. A single malt is the aged and unblended produce of just one cask from a given distillery – the best of them wondrous beyond words, and even the foot soldiers none too shabby. The golden rule at a tasting: don't spit. Some do, but don't – it's a waste, and not a pretty sight. A great show is made of half-filling a good and heavy plain crystal tumbler (essential) with a malt that retails at £200 a bottle, and then tipping it away. This, the smug chap in charge says, "prepares the glass". Before you can weep, the slugs start coming: close eyes, sniff, inhale, sip, sip more deeply, hold in the mouth, swirl it, chew it, let it glide down. On to the next (and they keep on getting better). Close eyes, sniff, inhale, gulp, bit trickles out of mouth, get it down you. Next one: cock an eye, snort, forget to inhale, down it in one. On to the next: wink dementedly, spill a fair deal, chuck it back, ask for a refill. There might be another eight or ten to come, and so on to the grand finale: find yourself unable to see, miss your mouth completely, sing a rude and rousing song with all your new best mates in the world, pass out with grace. ❖

A Cigar Is Just a Cigar

By Reg Gadney

Reg, a novelist and artist, smoked his first cigar
when he was seven years old

YOU RARELY SEE a miserable-looking cigar smoker. Not only that, but some well-known cigar smokers have lived to a great age. Churchill, of course, lived to 90: "I drink a great deal. I sleep a little, and I smoke cigar after cigar. That is why I am in 200% form." To say nothing of centenarian George Burns: "If I had taken my doctor's advice and quit smoking when he advised me to, I wouldn't have lived to go to his funeral."

Along with champagne and port, the cigar is a tool of celebration, hence its association with happiness, not misery. But cigar aficionados will rumble those out to flaunt their wealth, status and self-importance if they are seen brandishing a cigar the size of a bicycle pump. Resist ostentation – no smoke rings, no onanistic texting, no shouting for more champagne while smoking and no camping about with a cigar between the middle and index fingers. And don't smoke at weddings – or funerals (unless you can disguise it with crematorium smoke).

Cigar-smoking is also a contemplative pastime – this meditative act, coupled with the calming properties of nicotine, is a catalyst for thought. Plus, there's considerable oral gratification to enjoy. It's like Freud said: "Smoking is indispensable if one has nothing to kiss." You shouldn't be doing anything else when smoking but smoking, thinking or partaking in good conversation.

Like the smoker, you can tell a great deal about a cigar from its appearance. Look at the wrapper. If it's dark, the cigar should be sweet and full-bodied. A dark leaf shows that it has most likely stayed longer on the plant, benefiting from more sun. The wrapper should feel smooth

Oliver Wright/digitoli.com

and have the slightest of shines. Its body should give a little to a squeeze and yet hold its shape.

Cuban cigars usually offer the most magisterial flavours. Named after the *cicada*, a cigar-shaped Spanish beetle, cigars originated in Cuba long before Columbus showed up. Dominican fillings are milder, whereas Nicaraguan or Honduran varieties are among the spiciest. The best cigars offer a full flavour: first bitter and intense, then spicy, nutty or woody and cedar-like. The taste varies depending on whether smoked indoors or out, first thing in the morning or late at night, after a good meal or with some brandy, port or coffee.

Cuban cigars (namely Montecristos or Bolivars) keep the best. But even after a few weeks, they'll dry out if stored in the original box. To prevent this, use a humidor, a box-like container made of wood (say, cherry or maple) that offers 65-70% humidity at 70F. Don't try and economise by storing your cigars in the fridge. And never buy your cigars from the supermarket.

So to the glorious ritual of sparking and smoking. Best not to chew off the end and spit and mooch around like Clint Eastwood with one of those Toscanos clenched between your teeth. Instead, cut off the head of the cigar with a guillotine. Don't warm the cigar before lighting. Light it with a wooden match or butane lighter without letting the flame hit the cigar's centre; instead, move it round the edge and puff gently. Smoke slowly. Do you inhale? It's personal preference but usual to inhale a bit, not all. De Niro inhales, Eastwood never (and he would often be heard grumbling about having to smoke so much on Western sets). Certainly if you're a novice, don't pull too hard, or it will give you a heart attack. Or make you violently sick.

> **'Best not to chew the end off and spit and mooch around like Clint Eastwood with one of those Toscanos clenched between your teeth'**

It used to be considered bad form to smoke a cigar without removing the band first – the cigar band was once intended to protect the fingers when men sported white gloves for a big night out. Nowadays, nobody cares either way. If you do remove it, smoke the cigar for a short while so the gum of the wrapper is easy to remove, otherwise you may rip the wrapper. Avoid dipping the cigar into brandy or port, a trick said to have been invented by Churchill, who also dropped unfinished cigars in public for souvenir hunters to snap up, a habit that explains why his old butts still appear in auction rooms. Likewise, budding Clintons with aims on using the cigar tube for something beneath the desk and waist should heed Dr Freud: "A cigar is just a cigar." ❖

I Love Hangovers

By Simon Munnery

Simon is an alcoholic comic and chronic melancholic
with only one bollock

I HEAR THEM on the bus, the young with their tales of the night
before. They can hardly remember what happened, but this morning the
hangover and the pain of it provide the point of the story, the punchline:
we celebrate our own suffering. And why not? It's all we have.

Suffering is the primary social currency. If you haven't suffered, you
haven't lived. If you're suffering now, I'm with you, brother. Suffering is
your ticket to the human race. To whom do we tell our suffering? Not
our mothers, but our mates. Your mum doesn't want to know you are
hurting yourself.

We use so many phrases to describe the intoxication, which we then
hardly remember:

I was well gone; hammered; caned; rat-arsed; shit-faced; cunted;
totally boughed; tanked up; smashed; cranked up to the ninepins;
mashed; mullered; skidaddled; way tipsy; slaughtered; slightly
inebriated; kowlooned; dandelion boots off; ragtime Freddy....

– And how are you doing this morning?

– Oh, mate, don't ask... I can't tell you... really bad...

And so few to describe our suffering. Because suffering is only two
doors down from holy. No words will suffice.

Alcohol: one of the tools for change in this country, freeing the mind
from the chains that bind it. Ever had one of those nights when you're
out drinking and talking, talking and drinking – and someone is
listening. It's a good night, and then you're sick, but you carry on
drinking, then you're sick again, and it keeps happening over and over
and becomes like a routine in the end – drink, sick, drink, sick – then
you drink some sick by accident because you got it wrong, and you go
to sleep in a gutter – because you want to – and you wake up the next
day and your head's banging and your armpit smells like a kebab and

you look back on everything you said the night before and realise that what you'd been saying was completely and utterly brilliant? I have nights like that all the time...

It's a hangover
A remnant of the night before
A proof if one were needed
Of the continuousness of time
Don't worry it'll come back
Not immediately
But when it does
You'll regret it

The great advantage of the hangover is that you're in pain, so a little more won't make much difference. It's a good time to get on with chores: accountancy, washing up, e-mails, apologies. Washing up while hurting is a foretaste of old age.

Famously, there are three ways to avoid a hangover:

1. Don't drink. 2. Stay drunk. 3. Drink plenty of water before turning in

I never use option three. Why? Don't want to have to get up in the night. May have to anyway. When you are drunk enough that you must sleep, normally you've drunk so much that the thought of any more liquid is abhorrent. An alcoholic drink is firstly a drink; beer is mainly water; drinkers are *drinkers* first, alcoholics second; And drinking is the first pleasure. Drinkers miss their mums. And fear pissing the bed.

When I wake up, I like a cup of tea (milk, two sugars), a joint and a hot bath. If that doesn't work, I repeat the process. Sometimes it will be another 12 hours before I hit the sauce. I rarely have an aspirin. When I'm ready, I eat.

Dean Martin said he pitied sober people because when they wake up in the morning, that's the best they'll feel all day. He was wrong; sober people get on with their lives and experience the countless joys of interacting with the world with a clear head. The hangover sufferer struggles to do anything for half the day, eventually reaching a normal state before wasting his recovered strength on getting drunk again.

I drink for the hangover, to feel the pain of it, to live, for otherwise our lives would be a miserable ease. You have to conquer something. Everest's been done. So you conquer your own pain. It passes anyway, of course.❖

Edgerton Solpadeine Jason Shulman

2

Party and music

‘ The road to excess leads
to the palace of wisdom...
For we never know
what is enough
until we know what
is more than enough ’

William Blake

How to Be an Absolute Disgrace

By David Piper

David Piper is an inventor, performer, party organiser and writer who gets bored easily at parties. He has found that biting girls on the neck is far superior to small talk, and falling over spectacularly much more effective than big talk

THAT PRESSURE TO be perfect – it's all a bit much, isn't it? To behave, to perform, to turn up on time, to live within your means, to earn more, to be liked, to be successful... we are all constantly cowed by self-imposed restrictions. Aaargh! Responsibility to yourself? Help!

Disgrace, properly done, is a joyful act – so throw off that mantle of respectability, liberate yourself from the burden of good behaviour and spit in the eye of censure and approbation!

Sooner or later – if you are to avoid becoming a repressed bag of nerves – everyone must cross the line. If you do so unwittingly or unprepared, then I'm afraid you are done for. If, however, you can brush off the dust, ignore all damage, hold your head high, look disgrace squarely in the eye and say, "So what?" (oh, go on, "Fuck you!" if you want), then disgrace is your plaything and the broken rules your allies. Ignore it, or accept it. But never be ashamed, or it will smother you.

Get drunk, fall over. Scream abuse at a friend's partner, sleep with a friend's partner, bite someone, take off your clothes, assume inappropriate lewdness – in broad daylight, if possible. Fall over on the dancefloor, at a terribly important or fashionable party, while carrying a girl upstairs to bed. But make sure you fall with aplomb. Roar, jump up again, laugh, grab a drink, kiss the nearest lips, then retire with a wink, a huge grin and another twirl to fall over again elsewhere. So what if you knocked over a bottle of champagne, tore a dress, bruised an ankle? You're enjoying yourself immensely.

Faced with what is actually relatively harmless enjoyment, it is incredibly difficult to tut disapprovingly, unless you wish to appear the

Rebecca Lewis/Getty Images

very stereotype of a bitter spoilsport, a fun-hating, complaining old headmaster. Who can deny such spirit in a world of mediocrity, boredom, clones and social repression? You've released the silent pressure, loosened everyone's collars, become their vicarious prophet.

But for as long as you accept this as only half true, and that most people will actually think you a prize idiot, then you become that. If you don't care what they think (or at least give the impression of not caring), then you've got away with it. (The other method of getting away with it, of course, is to be powerful, rich or famous.)

This is not to say that, for the drink-spiller, prat-faller, pant-shitter, marriage-wrecker, friend-infuriator and scourge of hostesses, bouncers and the young and innocent, a quick "I'm so sorry" won't work wonders. But you can't actually acknowledge that what you've done is wrong – just that it may have caused some offence to the more uptight other party.

My ideal of disgrace is exemplified by the image of Errol Flynn in Hollywood Babylon, Kenneth Anger's exposé of Tinseltown's scandals. He is pictured at a party with a young fan, a girl of no more than 15.

She is obviously incredibly pleased to share the company of the star; she is also giving him a piggyback, and he is significantly larger than her. Her face is torn between the grimace of exertion (she dare not drop him), the necessity of not showing discomfort and the aforementioned pleasure. He is just having a sadistic whale of a time. Look what fun the bastard's having! What a gas! Silly girl! Of course, he's an absolute creep who couldn't care less about humiliating a young girl if he found it fun. But the fact is, it is fun (partly because he's being such a bastard), and by plunging headlong into the awfulness of the whole thing, he somehow gets away with it.

> **❛Fall over on the dancefloor, at a terribly important or fashionable party, while carrying a girl upstairs to bed❜**

But we can forget modern scandal here, which is largely manufactured by the press and quite rarely proper disgrace. Likewise, when on a Saturday night, every town centre in Britain is flooded with those incredibly proud of their boob-flashing, vomiting idiocy, I urge sophistication and inventiveness in your disgrace. At least there are still politicians and judges specifically bred for amusing, inappropriate, career-destroying sexual indiscretions. Every time I read of another caught flashing on a train or masturbating under his robes in court, I feel the world's axis is back in proper alignment.

The opprobrium of those around you must be stretched to its very limits, and you must draw your strength from it. Do you want a reputation as a respectable, compliant mouse, or a fireball of impulsive, self-assured, devil-may-care independence? Go on – bite that bottom! ❖

The Heavenly Virtues of Outrageous Hosts

By Fleur Britten

Fleur once hosted a fancy-breast party, thereby earning full
entitlement to make a right tit of herself

THE OUTRAGEOUS HOST (OH) is hedonism's hero. Gathering
people together to drink, dance, sing, laugh and love – orchestrating
group highs – provides the antidote to grim reality. It's what we have to
look forward to in life. All of you must throw legendary parties so that
others throw competitively legendary parties in return. Why? Because
the fire must never be allowed to go out.

The key to creating a legendary night is encouraging the unexpected.
Now, you obviously can't plan the unexpected, but you can leave the
door open to it. Cue our friend the hedonist – our trusty risk-taker and
gatekeeper to the Other Side. You can contrive a wild party all you like
with, say, key-swapping and bowlfuls of class As, but if you don't invite
hedonists, it's just a networking event. Then, to fill up space, summon
the easy and the pretty – one makes good gossip, the other, good photos.
(For yet more unpredictability, invite mutual grudge-bearers and
harbourers of dark secrets, and get everyone exceedingly amorous.)

Next, pick an occasion, any occasion. National Potato Day would do –
occasions create hype, and hype creates conversation. And then – just
like that – your party becomes a "topic". And topics hit the airwaves.
Before you know it, gatecrashers are sniffing hungrily – and that's the
first sign of a mad party. Love thy gatecrashers (and invite the
neighbours – it keeps the police at bay. As one neighbour said: "Nothing
makes you more tolerant of a neighbour's noisy party than being there.")

Now you need to keep the party buoyant. Throw in a fancy-dress theme
so guests can inhabit more interesting personalities than their own. You –
as the star, the party's engine – must be the most outrageously dressed of
all. Think Elton John (well, not quite) – fantasy flamboyance galvanises
everyone into the game. Then your job is to connect. Big up friends when
introducing them: try "Meet TV's Hotlegs Holly!" for Holly the runner. It

charges the ego (unbridled parties require unfettered superegos), creates intrigue and is, of course, a little private joke for you to watch unfold.

Obviously, you need to ship in the swearing juice. For a little *je ne sais quoi*, bulk-buy the more psychoactive drinks – absinthe, tequila and those peculiar Chinese spirits containing snakes and lizards and God knows what – in industrial quantities because the OH never runs dry. To really harness the collective joy, consider passing around the Cup of Love (pink champagne and MDMA is one such communal cocktail). A Boring Note of Caution: hold onto the Cup at all times – you don't want a novice taking more than their fair share and embarrassing you. You could supply a few judicious carb-loaded snacks, but don't go diluting the drunkenness with a lavish spread. Things stay way too polite with lots of nice food.

And while the host Must Not Pass Out, don't expect anybody else to be sensible. The OH is sympathetic to casualties – if you want people on the edge, you have to accept that a few will fall off. Your largest concern – providing nobody dies – is being remembered as the OH when guests are lying face-down in the flowerbed. The trick is to create standout incidents. Establish a laughing-gas grotto – simply buy a cream whipper and the accompanying nitrous-dioxide chargers and fill balloons with the

Miko Miroslav Vranic

stuff (buy plenty: it's one charger per two-minute hit of pure, wild hilarity). Or for dinner parties, why not halve the ratio of crockery and cutlery to people and double the alcohol – cosy, *non*, when the Couple Least Likely have to share a plate?

Encourage regressive behaviour to loosen up guests – try channelling an alcoholic child's birthday party. Fill a props box with party hats, stick-on 'taches, fly swats for patting bottoms and limbo tools (read: social crutches). Dress the set with objects of curiosity – perhaps some phallic fruits, body paints (remove clothes first) or musical instruments (it needn't get too technical – saucepans for drums, bottles for flutes and tennis-racket guitars). If you've invited the right crowd, an absurd, sticky jam session will ensue in no time.

The OH loves every guest absolutely: this takes considerable public-spiritedness. If Jackson Pollock pissed on your fire, as he did on Peggy Guggenheim's; if Princess Margaret brought out her naughty salt; if your bedroom becomes a seething sin bin, so be it. Book a cleaning lady and banish your rubber gloves to the props box – infamy is to be encouraged. As keepers of the flame, social benefactors merit unconditional popularity. You will proceed directly to heaven.❖

Nonstop Hedonism
By Tiffanie Darke

Tiffanie is an almost breathless magazine editor
and adrenalin lover

THE NO-BOUNDARY LIFESTYLE. This is dangerous over a long period, resulting in total exhaustion, burnout and other boring, non-hedonistic consequences. Over the short term, however, even up to a couple of years, it's highly achievable, hugely productive and allows you to extract every last ounce of juice out of life. You need a job that feeds off your playtime, and playtime that feeds off your job. I had the perfect one: a lifestyle journalist. Parties every night, launches every day, a constant stream of "meetings" conducted over breakfasts, lunches, teas, drinks and dinners (why is it we can't meet people without ingesting something?) and – most importantly – a single, childless lifestyle with no responsibilities to anybody except myself (and not much of that, either). Here's what I learnt on the way about how to do it:

The Party Friend/Confessor
First, you can't do this alone. When things get hectic, you've gotta talk. Your party friend/confessor is like therapy – you need somebody to be utterly complicit in your behaviour, someone you can text at 4am with the latest gossip, and at 9am when you're close to tears. They need to accompany you out when all your friends have passed out, understand your job, contribute to it, sympathise with you when you're running on empty and meet you for a drink to refuel. Your mind is spinning in a 24/7 lifestyle and you need someone in there with you to share it. Otherwise, what's the point? NB: this cannot be a boyfriend/girlfriend. They will expect you to spend "quality time alone with them", which is not part of the work/play nonstop lifestyle. It's distracting, it's time out and it's not allowed. Short-term dalliances, on the other hand, are most definitely allowed. A woman, after all, cannot live on bread alone…

Sleep

An annoying diversion that unfortunately needs acknowledging every now and then. All manner of things can be ingested to avoid sleep, and plenty of counter-diversions can be found to relegate its need, but eventually, it's going to tap you on the shoulder and go, "Ahem". So take it wherever you can find it, but never instead of something else. It's your last priority, when there's nothing better going on. I also had one rule that kept me totally sane: Nothing Changes After 6am. Honestly. Call that cab and head home, because it doesn't get any prettier from there on in.

Health and Fitness

You need to be match-fit. I trained with a personal trainer for a couple of hours a week and cycled everywhere (see Transport). In addition, observing a health-obsessed, nutrition-aware diet (slow-burning carbs and loads of fruit and veg) half the time will allow you to cope with those days when you're so hungover that all you can imagine is a plate of pasta, a bottle of red wine and a tray of cream cakes. Food is fuel, and you need quality stuff because energy is vital to the 24/7 lifestyle. Porridge in the morning can do an awful lot for your GI balance. Get those carbs in at lunchtime – they only slow you right down at dinner. And every time somebody's picking up the tab for a meal, take the fillet steak or steamed sea bass. And start with a freshly squeezed juice – it's quite possible to get those five a day down you on somebody else's bill.

Transport

Drive at least two nights a week. This stops you drinking, thus facilitating sleeping, being on the ball for the work side of things and coping with your mounting taxi bill. The rest of the time, get on your bike. It keeps you fit, burns off the alcohol and contributes to the idea that you are always moving, never at rest.

Attitude

Never give up. Never say die. Having a bad moment? Move on to the next one. It's like an evening of parties – if you arrive at one and it's deathly dull, do a twirl and walk right back out the door and on to the next one. When the moment looks like it's going to fold – sleep's tapping you on the shoulder, the sofa's calling your name, time out

Andrea Pistolesi/Getty Images

seems like a nice option – laugh in their faces and divert yourself. The thrill of doing nothing will soon dissolve. Keep moving, mentally and physically, and all those boundaries you thought existed will be notable by their absence. Life will just be a series of possibilities, all there for the taking. And the wildest, freshest white-water rush of experience.❖

Party SOS: How to Rescue a Shite Night

By Fleur Britten

Fleur wrote Debrett's Etiquette for Girls; however, following extensive fieldwork, she is of the resolute opinion that there is no place for perfect manners at parties

JOKE: TWO FRIENDS, Nwankwo and Kelechi, go to a party; the theme, "moods". The host throws open the door. "Welcome, welcome, my friends! Ah…" his voice trails. "Tell me, what have you come as?" Nwankwo, entirely naked, with his one-eyed worm swimming in a bowl of custard, replies: "Ah'm fuckin' dis custid." Kelechi, also naked, save a pear on his manstick, says: "Ah've come in dis pear."

The moral of the joke is that bad moods should be left at home – parties are no substitute for therapy. But some people will not listen. We have all experienced that heart-sink moment on arrival at a shitty pity-party, miserablists at every turn and the wrong side of an hour-long hike across the city. But shitty is a state of mind. By assuming the spirit of a superhero and applying the right party correctives, everyone should soon be bowing at the altar of the bender. Here's how to smash the in-case-of-dire-party emergency glass.

Social Evils: First, arm yourself with a repertoire of taste-free jokes, as above, for when buttonholed by crashing bores. You'll soon be left in peace. Parties get off on controversy. It's like party- and quote-hag Oscar Wilde said, "Hear no evil, speak no evil and you'll never be invited to a party," so be sure to talk up taboo (necrophilia, defecation or incest will divert attention like a car crash). Social fireworks, stirring and fun-poking not only make the night go faster, they rip off the comfort blanket of insipid niceness – a barrier to wanton freedom.

Bring Your Own Entertainment Equip yourself with plenty of intoxicants – imperative, even if on the programme – then you get to enjoy the spectacle of others' self-destruction. Next, mobilise an entourage (because you can't place all hope in chance) – preferably drag queens, buskers and friendly-looking tourists collected en route – think experimental. All on your lonesome? Be the bartender, you'll soon be the centre of attention. Plus, you can amuse yourself by sedating the worst perpetrators of self-pity, while ensuring that you get your fair share.

Charm the Pants Off Others Salute all other guests, friends or otherwise, and be atomic – only stay in the same place if playing musical statues. Leave the clutches of your friends and sidle up to strangers to take them down that Yellow Brick Road with indecorous yarns (NB: gross misrepresentation of the facts is permissible if yarn unravels into a sorry non-starter). You may find, though, that all this is not enough to encourage pant-dropping. That's because this can only be done with reciprocal disclosure: ie you too, or really, you first. A bit of nudity-induced nervous giggling/a full-blown sex scandal is an excellent distraction from guests banging on about malevolent mothers-in-law/malfunctioning Biros etc.

FLIRT (so important, it needs capitals) With or without intent. With girls and with boys. Because it flatters and disarms and charges the atmosphere and encourages ego trips. Plus, it might lead to a snog in a cupboard. Consider the more extreme strategy of "smash and grab" – just make a lunge for them. They'll soon forget about whatever it was.

Up-dressing Invent a "concept costume" (ie rubbish and spontaneous) by appropriating the host's shower cap/feather duster/pudding bowl. The sight instantly encourages people to get over themselves. As a concept, it needs a show-name – your outfit is a social catalyst and thus deserves an introduction. Once upon a time there was a P-themed party that two friends went to as a pair of parallel lines – nice and silly, see? It might not make for world-changing conversation, but it does encourage mirth. And mirth maketh people fall in love.

Party Tricks – When All Else Fails Applying lipstick with your cleavage = 7 points. Applying it to someone else's lips = 10 points. Tying a cherry stalk with your tongue = 3 points. Tying a cherry stalk with your tongue in someone else's mouth = 12 points. Serenading a stranger = 7 points. Flipping your eyelids = -1 point. Amateur magic = bit tragic, but if slick, better than silence. Keep it quick for 4 points. Passing out in own vomit = *nul points*. Ditto laying a turd in the kitchen. Changing all clocks and watches to a much earlier time so that everyone stays much later = very many points (try "Nice watch – gizzus a look"). Or, if a party simply refuses to warm up, move all timepieces forward and be done with it ("My, is that the time?").❖

Dance Like Everyone's Watching

By Tom Stubbs

Tom is a writer, stylist and ageing shuffler who
occasionally drops a bit of "nouveau mannequin"
and a few "capoeira taxi hails" in his leisure time

"DANCE LIKE THERE'S nobody watching," goes the pseudo-edifying
adage. I firmly advise the contrary. Total abandonment of hang-ups and
embarrassment is to the detriment of the dancefloor – and your image.
Dancing is about letting go in a good, micro-managed way, not just
letting go.

The theory

Dance is a physical expression of music appreciation entrenched in
sexual inclinations; a hedonistic activity geared to sensory and physical
satisfaction. We frequently dance just to follow protocol. It's supposed
to be fun, but there are many layers. Good dancing is liberating, stylish
and attractive. Bad manoeuvres are a physical utterance of disharmony,
a statement of naffness and look plain rubbish.

The herd

Forget what those planktons are doing down the disco. They are mere
backdrop fodder for the real stroke-pullers. Throw away their
homogenised pamphlet of dance rhetoric and start again with your own
gratification in mind.

Conception

A manifesto is required: basic shapes hewn from taste, physicality and
self-expression. Acquire a handful of stances that represent suitably and
test at home: you're going to look silly anyway. Make a phrase from two
or three moves, maybe with a postural exclamation at the end of each
bar. A few "care in the community" moves are good, but must be

pinned down with good architectural solids. Make sure you can feel it with conviction.

Procedure

Don't give a jot when you step out, armed with an agenda in attitude form. Dancing is daft, so there's no margin for shyness. Strut from the sidelines like you've invented a new genre, then deliver it with blissful calm. As things hot up, drop in the odd concerned frown or manic glare. You're off.

Gauge the floor

Is the music any good? If not, I say stop. Stand stoic as a protest if you feel so inclined. What are the other revellers doing? Best not to join in. Get inspired and say a limb- and beat-based sentence out loud. If it feels good, say it again. In different dialects. Recite a whole speech on the subject of the song that's playing, but all in dance form. Easy, right?

Inebriation

Inevitably, one is going to fall under the influence. My advice is to roll with it. Allow stumbles to translate into jazz-dance metaphors. When coked up, drink and smoke heavily and try and relax your jaw. E, or Michael Douglas, as MDMA is sometimes known, is probably the best thing to dance on, but get too relaxed and you'll come over like a Christian supply teacher at sports day. Skipping like the new rector at harvest festival might just do trick, though. K slides are like teleporting from one spot to another, so try a few Jacksonesque moves. Dropped your drugs? Devise an L-shaped little blues dance that utilises head-down action, and sweep across the dance floor. Perhaps best just to have a couple of white wines.

Now you're motoring

Once up and running and things feel spot-on, you'll note a feeling of subtle euphoria. This is the zone you're after. When I rolled with a group of dedicated Balearic shufflers, we'd enter a blissful territory where, at the zenith, the crew resembled a gaggle of simpleton halfway-housers on a day trip to the seaside. Total release – showing the world what you and your spars are about; sharing, but not allowing entry; exposing your vulnerabilities, but with such bravado, you're immune.

Untitled from the series 'Come and be my Baby'
Courtesy of Lucy Levene & 511 gallery, New York

It's this relaxed openness that fast-tracks the sex thing. Of course, dancing is all about sex, but nobody's going to admit it. Advanced carefree foolishness suggests you're off the Richter scale in the sack. Calm assuredness while performing an obviously sexualised movement is a little like wanking in public. Making eye contact with someone is similar to shafting eye-to-eye with a detached determination that comes when two right filthy sods lock together.

The dancefloor is a mass open audition. Nobody wants to look keen, but there's a fair bit of "Clock what I'm capable of, matey". This is why it's such fun. Check every CV in the room, put out a few invites and ask for a couple of re-sees – no desperate open invitations, mind. Remember, everyone's watching.❖

Rule Like a Drag Queen

By Jodie Harsh

Jodie is London's fiercest drag queen and the
self-crowned Alternative Queen of England

DRAG IS A BIG "fuck you" in the face of small-mindedness. As thrills
go, the ego trip of turning every living head onto you, while dressed as
the wrong gender and acting like a vicar's worst nightmare, is up there
with ruling the world. Drag is the ultimate antidote to mediocrity and
boredom: a taboo for the taking, a trip of gratuitous rebellion. And
alongside the joy of alienating the mainstream, there is privilege
aplenty to reap from the fawning underground – free drinks, guest-list
entry, sexual attention from "tranny fuckers" (glass-closeted straight
guys up for "girls") and paparazzi-style fuss from anybody with a
camera. In fact, once you start getting paid to go to parties, there's a
whole new career in it. Women can be queens, too – look at where it's
got Amy Winehouse and Jordan.

Feared and adored in equal measure, the drag star carries some
major currency – and it pays in pleasure: filthy, egotistical, self-
reverential pleasure. When in drag, you're an instant nightlife celeb,
automatically propelled to the top of the high-heeled hierarchy of VIP-
dom. Dragging up affords free entry into a super-race, because walking
down the street in heels and lipstick takes real balls. Here's how:

1. Create a character Honeys, your mirror mantra is, "No such
thing as too much". Drag is a parody, so overemphasise feminine
attributes with over-the-top shock. Safety is for pussies. Achieve fantasy
hair with a big, backcombed wig (as giant as you can make it without
the aid of scaffolding, and pinned down to avoid slippage in the event
of a scrap). Make-up should be thickly yet expertly smothered, as if a
rainbow has exploded tastefully on your face. Go for double fake lashes,
extreme lip liner and contoured cheekbones as cutting as your attitude.

Your frock should deliver oversexualised "glamma", your big, spiked heels referencing the phallic surprise beneath your dress. The finishing touch should always be too much. Now admire your reflection – who is this beast? Give her a name with attitude and wit: for example, Sheila Blige, Celine Neon, Pantherella.

2. Walk the walk Practise your strut before you leave the house. Walk like a model with dainty steps (as if restrained by a pencil skirt) and swing those arms, sway those hips, and cross one foot over the other like a cat. Don't fall over. If you do, roll around on the floor and swing your hair around like Beyoncé as if it were all on purpose. When ready to leave, don't take a coat – you don't want to stand in the cloakroom queue with the proletariat.

3. Act fierce Drag is part appearance, part superbitch. Hands should be firmly on hips 90% of the time. Mimic poses from fashion magazines without any trace of irony. Employ the art of "vogueing" (basically, bitcho attitude; see the cult movie Paris Is Burning for ammunition) and "throw shade" at anybody in your way (act like a bitch, armed with a biting snarl and acid-tongued put-downs). If mean enough, you may want to "read" a fellow queen. This involves picking on your opponent's deepest insecurities (a big nose or a polyester outfit, for example) to humiliate them in a public slanging match. That will teach her not to buy the same wig as you. If a friend (or foe) leans in for an air-kiss (NB: never make skin contact when social kissing), pull away before the second one and just smile blankly. That's fierce.

4. Exhibit The world is your stage, the public your audience, their shameless stares your fuel. Be high camp: throw up your arms, toss back your head and laugh demonstrably ("Camp is an exaggeration of character," as Susan Sontag wrote). Smoke with grand drama and only ever accept champagne (drink through straws to avoid lipstick-smudging). Reapply lip gloss more than is necessary, and if you must dance (strictly a plebian activity), be sure to pose in front of your handheld mirror. When being photographed, always stand on the outside with your friends on your left, thus ensuring your name appears first in the picture caption. To pose, stand side-on to the camera, chin up to the shoulder, and drop one hip (à la Liz Hurley). Surround

Model: Ll Kenny, New York City Adolfo 'Spyder' Gallela

yourself with fabulous people – though none quite as fabulous as you, the queen bee – and employ an intern to trot after you and manage your diary. Just remember – you're fucking royalty. At least, you could be, if you play your cards right.❖

How to Be a Hedonist Until You Die

By Kate Spicer

Kate is a journalist and anthropologist who
has lived for many years among the
mysterious peoples of the train/cane tribe

LET US PRESUME that you aren't the sort of rarefied Epicurean
hedonist who craves Proust and 19th-century philosophers. Perhaps
you should be. This model is unlikely to kill you. Most of us, however,
are probably closer to the knee-jerk, gimme-gimme hedonist who
chases buzzes, hits, highs and orgasms. If so, you will be laid wide open
to an array of health-damaging, life-threatening activities. But hedonism
should accompany you through a long and interesting life, as opposed
to leading you on a choke chain towards oblivion. Time, then, to
consider healthy hedonism: managing your vices so they don't kill you
until you want them to. Because nothing puts a dampener on things like
a premature death, especially if it's your own.

Premature death, sickness, psychological meltdown, dire financial
straits, flaky nails… all are common and pesky side effects of poorly
administered hedonism. This is the difference in lifestyle between, say,
George Melly (who dropped dead at 80 after a life of steady genius and
excess) and Rolling Stones founder member Brian Jones (who died at
27, preserving his beauty and legend, but missing out on the obvious
perks of avoiding a rock'n'roll DOD).

Rich and famous hedonists know exactly what to do: simply book in
for a nice long, healthy stay in a Swiss clinic. The less time- and cash-
rich among us must recreate the rehab environment with what is
commonly known as the feast/famine, train/cane, spa/bar or
cocaine/yogi lifestyle. Healthy hedonism is about interspersing excess
and pleasure with a wholesome lifestyle. Moments of micro-rehab are
essential: take the train to somewhere quiet and boring to sleep, read
nourishing books, take the air and nurture your knackered mind, body

and soul right back to party-fit health.

Even while engaged in fun, the hedonist can still make healthy choices. Let's take the mundane, up-all-night dirty sex and getting high on a Sunday night/Monday morning scenario. Uppers followed by downer-induced heart failure is a really bad look. The healthy hedonist's way is to drink water between the booze, to use soothing but safe herbs/sex/pub trips to take the sting out of any comedown, or – and this is where the healthy hedonist really trumps the hardcore, fuck-it-all caner – they will be so physically fit they don't actually get bad comedowns or guilt complexes any more.

Going to work on hangovers and comedowns is very, very ageing. Healthy hedonists work for themselves so they can take off recreational days whenever required, or they have the confidence and status to abuse their position and take sickies or be at "important meetings" if necessary. The healthy hedonist has good sense and knows that work, frankly, ain't that important. Rocking up at the office feeling shit is no badge of honour, it's extremely stupid. Suffering shouldn't be part of a hedonistic lifestyle, unless you're one of those silly sado-masochists – anything beyond a little light bondage is generally the turf of the unhealthy hedonist.

Aldous Huxley got it right: "How desperately bored, in spite of their grim determination to have a Good Time, the majority of pleasure-seekers really are." Huxley's experimentation with psychedelics, described in his seminal essay, The Doors of Perception, provided some extremely useful reasoning. Using hedonism to explore new sensations, untap mental states or to provoke deeper spirituality will always be healthier than hanging your face over the bar for the sake of getting out of it. Any mindless habit is calcifying to the human spirit. Even if you cannot write a searching essay on mind expansion, it is wise to avoid unquestioning repetition. Rotate your hedonistic thrills, take time off from them, cultivate new pastures, swap hard drugs for adrenalin and the pursuit of extreme sports (physical challenges also stimulate the body's pleasure receptors). Lord Byron swam the Hellespont and wrote poems in addition to his laudanum habit, womanising, incest and closet homosexuality (although his healthy hedonist credentials are a bit rubbish, given that he died of a bad cold at the age of 36).

This breed of hedonism is not about being good; it shouldn't sound like brown-bread, high-fibre naughtiness (although a healthy digestive

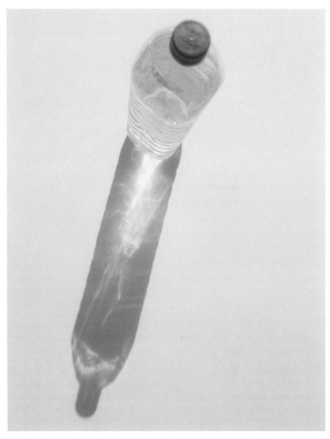

Doable/Getty Images

tract will make life eminently more pleasurable). It's about looking after the needs of the whole person. Nutritious food, choosing ideology over the blackness of nihilism (or worse, just complete intellectual numbness), plenty of water, sleep, intellectual stimulation, creative and physical activity, love, fresh fruit and an avoidance of the destructive grip of addiction are musts. Otherwise hedonism is just terribly hard work, and doesn't that defeat the purpose? ❖

A Hedonist's Record Collection

By Alex Needham

Alex is a Guardian arts journalist whose own collection bears the scars of working for Smash Hits, The Face and NME, making it possibly the world's only collection to include the first Libertines 7in, rare French filter disco white labels and three 5ive albums

THE INFAMOUS TRIUMVIRATE of sex, drugs and rock'n'roll (and indeed wine, women and song) says it all: a night out without music is like seeing in two dimensions – it's all a bit flat. Music may well be the ultimate mood-enhancer – as you fantasise you're one of Queens of the Stone Age when you're actually called Colin. But to get the most out of music, it needs to be experienced at high volume and with as many like-minded people as possible, preferably with a pint of lager in one hand and someone's underclothes in the other.

> **'If you play them at a party and nobody dances, you should a) insist on a refund for this book and b) really be more careful which parties you attend'**

Since the first caveman banged two mammoth's tusks together (or something), music has been made to entertain a group, not to be piped into one person's brain via some tinny white earplugs. So we counterbalance the unnatural insularity of the way we consume music now by doing something at the other extreme. Homo sapiens are hard-wired with the desire to dance – it's an inescapable chemical reaction to hearing a rocking tune. In the same way, we'll always find it liberating to sing loudly and en masse, which is why festivals (and even weddings) speak directly to our pleasure-seeking caveman instinct.

It's like Madonna said: music makes the people come together. It's the catalyst for our good times, the common ground we can find with complete strangers, the thing that makes us slip our individuality and

Irene Barros

unite in shared joy. And that's how great music feels when it really hits you – that you're being lifted out of yourself and taken over by something to which you're happy to relinquish control. You can just about enjoy a club with terrible music if the company's right, but even the most Ecstasy-fuelled group of ravers will only have a moderate amount of fun in a room with no stereo.

So which records stir us most effectively? What is in a hedonist's music collection? Records that engage with the body rather than the brain – you don't want a complicated lyric when you're trying to get lost in music, never mind a ballad, or something with "interesting" time signatures. What you want is an amazing bassline to suck you onto the dancefloor, drums that make your heart beat faster, some element of repetition (which helps you to get further into that trancelike state) and something simple that you can chant along to – preferably some words endorsing the pursuit of kicks.

The ultimate hedonist's anthem is probably Iggy Pop's Lust for Life, originally released in 1978, and which, even 18 years later, sat on the soundtrack to Trainspotting, a film, after all, about a bunch of death-tripping junkies. Lust for Life's opening drum tattoo is an adrenalin rush made audible, the longer-than-you-expect intro allows you ample time to immerse yourself in the brilliant mixture of art rock and rockabilly Iggy Pop. And while it plays, the music envelops you in an eternal present. There's nothing but Iggy and the moment, and the physical, chemical and emotional effect it's having on you. It's a reaffirmation of your lust for life – that's what pop music can do.

Here are some other random songs that follow the rules above, which are found in the hedonist's battered and well-thumbed record collection (picture every CD sleeve cracked, every album cover harbouring traces of marijuana and an iPod held together with rubber bands). If you play them at a party and nobody dances, you should a) insist on a refund for this book and b) really be more careful which parties you attend.

I Feel Love **by Donna Summer**
A relentlessly juddering bassline, almost wordless, orgasmic cries, and a record that immerses you in it completely.

Cigarettes and Alcohol **by Oasis**
An exhilarating, communal celebration of ripping your boring existence a new arsehole and realising that "you've got to make it happen".

Rocker **by Alter Ego**
An awesome pile-up of the nastiest synthesizer sounds ever, irresistible and heavy enough to compel everyone from Girls Aloud fans to heavy-metal freaks to unite on the dancefloor.

Kashmir **by Led Zeppelin**
The most hedonistic records feature at least one build and release of tension. This is nothing but build and release – and it lasts eight minutes. Like participating in a dinosaur orgy.

Metal Guru **by T.Rex**
"Just like a silver-studded, sabre-tooth dream," sings Marc Bolan. We might not understand what he means on a rational level, but the music ensures that we get it, all right.❖

The DJing Game

By Tabitha from Queens of Noize

Queens of Noize, namely Tabitha Denholm and Mairead Nash,
are the shonky girl DJ duo who double-handedly gave the art
of DJing a shakedown with their shambolic sets, devil-may-care
attitude and eye-catching pants

HAVE YOU EVER lost entire afternoons tipsily singing along to your
favourite records in daft hats? If so, DJing is the job for you. You will not
only get paid for this carry-on in ready cash, but you will be serviced
regularly with free booze. When armed with a record box, the trials of
queuing, paying and tolerating moody door people all fade into distant
memory. In fact, all sense of reality can start to slide once you surrender
to the nocturnal world of colourful characters and nameless lounges.*
And when you wake up at noon, it is not with the guilt of a day lost, but
with the knowledge of a job well done, and a glorious, if hazy, memory
of puppeteering the crowd into euphoric communion.

Previously, boys became DJs because they couldn't dance, preferring
to closet themselves in smoky bedrooms practising on their trophy
equipment. Showmanship consisted of a sweaty man making a Y sign
with his body and pointing. Not cool. Nobody wants to see a pretentious
twit in oversized headphones making life-or-death decisions about the
next "groove". We say showmanship is crowd-surfing a *piñata* into a
mosh pit to be torn to pieces, or leading 5,000 high Danes in a session
of strip aerobics (really). The golden rule is, IT'S MEANT TO BE FUN.
DJing took a wrong turn when people forgot this – now you've just got
to let it all hang out. Dance like a loon, and the crowd dances with you.
Then you just need to know how to play a shambolic set. Try this:

Learn by Doing A passion for music is imperative, so you should
already have the records. Don't be intimidated by the equipment – a
chimp could master a crossfader. Just dive in: the never-mind-the-gaps
school of DJing is very forgiving.

Form a Double Act One girl dressed like a flamenco dancer flailing her arms about is cringeful, two makes an act (NB: more than two becomes impractical). People are drawn to strong bonds – they want to be in your gang. Once you give your partnership a daft name, it becomes an entity, and you're off.

Imbibing[+] Rock'n'roll DJing and copious amounts of alcohol go hand in hand. We recommend slippery nipples (shots of sambuca floating dangerously on a bed of Baileys). When enjoyed in brisk succession, they have a narcotic effect comparable to PCP.

What to Play Get the balance right. Bring some new sonic treats – there's no excuse not to, when you can download everything for free. Plus, a good remix does the DJing for you. It's always satisfying to have the same stuff in your bag as the serious boys, but a whiff of fromage encourages silliness. Which we all like. If you give the audience everything they want, it's like having too many chocolates – it makes you sick. But don't overindulge yourself on the sonic outer limits either, because it goes against the golden rule, IMTBFun.

Happy Accidents If something "unconventional" happens, embrace it; take it to the crowd. Occasionally, you will find yourself in a fix. If this happens, there are a few get-out clauses. If a track really bombs, whip it off the decks, snap it in two and throw it to the baying mob. They love that. If you spill booze on the mixer, immediately implicate the drunken twit who requested funk earlier (venue owners tend to take this very seriously). Falling off podiums, decks, tall people etc is inevitable – embrace your war wounds as reminders of the good times had.

DJ Crimes Worst of all is the "DJ nod", which can be traced back to the "rock nod" lineage, perpetrated by guitarists in boring prog-rock bands who would screw up their eyes and move their heads up and down to indicate being lost in a vibe. This sickeningly contrived piece of body language is intended to give the impression that the nodder has exclusive access to secret musical knowledge. Also, don't get all hip-speak and start saying "spinning" or "dropping" – "playing" works fine.

Pulling the Plug Never finish playing when the bouncer asks you – it looks like you don't care. Always wait until they pull the plug. You owe it to the people.

Occupational Hazards *Drug Addiction – if you find yourself spending a disproportionately large amount of time in nameless lounges, particularly in the morning, then maybe it's time to get help.*

+Alcoholism – this is to be avoided as it takes all the fun out of drinking.❖

Your Life Will Be Better if You Play Guitar

By Will Hodgkinson

At 34, Will Hodgkinson cadged lessons from the Byrds' Roger McGuinn and the Smiths' Johnny Marr, and drove his wife to near insanity with horrific versions of You Can't Always Get What You Want. His book, Guitar Man, tells the whole sorry story

WHETHER SEARCHING FOR base pleasures or spiritual depths, the guitar will help you. The enlightened way of approaching this instrument is to play it for hours on end in the knowledge that you will, ultimately, achieve nothing whatsoever, thereby reaching a nirvana-like state of pure being. But it can help you get laid, too.

For two decades, the guitar was my enemy. I resented its rebellious image and ability to transform invisible losers into stardust-sprinkled sex gods. More than once during adolescence, I found myself sitting around a campfire with a few beers, a few friends and thoughts of romance running through my head. I would be chatting up a pretty girl and, after a while, the possibility of a long and happy night would present itself. Then some chisel-jawed, long-haired idiot would start strumming Hotel California, and all of a sudden, the girl was by his side and not mine, and once again, the evening's entertainment consisted of a Scrabble marathon with the school's volunteer library monitor. And his mother.

Who wouldn't hate these six-stringed aphrodisiacs, given the mental cruelty and sexual frustration they have caused? As a teenager, every boy I knew seemed to be picking up a guitar and, a few months later, knocking out the opening riff to Pinball Wizard or a clumsy rendition of Lay Lady Lay as a clutch of flaxen-haired beauties swayed dreamily in far-out communion by his feet. Not wishing to be the last to join the party, I stayed away, only to observe one formerly untouchable friend after another swap restraining orders for girlfriends. Amazingly, this has been going on since the 14th century. Way back in 1393, a tract reported on the growing problem of drunken, unruly abbots playing the

Mischa Photo Ltd/Getty Images

gittern – a four-course precursor to the guitar – "to geter the stynkyng love of damyselis".

The stynkyng love of damyselis is just one colour in a rainbow of joys to be had in return for putting in the practice. If you don't mind being poor until fame kicks in, you don't even have to work. A few years ago, I interviewed Blur guitarist Graham Coxon, and I mentioned that it seemed strange how musicians are described as lazy, given the dedication needed to play an instrument well. "But it is lazy, isn't it?" Coxon replied. "You sit there in your flat for days on end, doing nothing more than strumming your guitar, making cups of tea and smoking cigarettes, and you end up becoming rich and famous for it." He gave a resigned sigh and lit another cigarette.

The guitar is gloriously tainted by the glamour of rebellion. But even if you don't become a rock star, it can still justify your purpose on the planet and help you to swap the boring, straight world for a more exciting itinerant existence. People who would otherwise be classed as bums become bohemians by slinging a guitar over their shoulders. Take the case of Teddy Paige. The former Memphis session musician worked at the legendary Sun Studios in the 1960s. Then, in 1972, he disappeared. It was reported that he had fallen victim to a suicide cult, but the truth was stranger: he had travelled to Europe to become a medieval troubadour, complete with tights, pointy shoes, a lute, a guitar and a steak-only diet. He took medieval authenticity a little too far in 2003 when he attacked his neighbour with a 3ft sword, resulting in his subsequent incarceration at a high-security psychiatric institute, but until then, the guitar had been Paige's passport to a life of unbridled freedom.

It was only at the age of 34 – by which point I was too old, too grumpy and too married to entertain rock-star fantasies – that I got over my resentment of the guitar to realise that by playing it for its own sake, you might just change your life for the better. I bought a cheap acoustic, got lessons from a few of my favourite players and trawled the Deep South to understand how the guitar – cheap, transportable and easy to master in a basic fashion – allowed that blighted part of the world to give birth to blues, soul and rock'n'roll; the cornerstones of popular Western music. Ultimately, I learnt that its real purpose is to offer both an escape from reality and an enrichment of it. Somewhere between cosmic freedom and responsibility to the people you love lays the answer to life. The guitar is a good place to go in search of it. ❖

How to Survive Festivals Without Really Trying

By Bill Brewster

Bill is a DJ, writer and *bon viveur*, although not usually at the same time

IN THE 1960s, when the festival was still in its infancy and it wasn't unusual for Hells Angels to beat you to death for liking the Grateful Dead and dressing as a marigold (proof that we have much to learn from this maligned era), the festival experience was probably the nearest you could come to re-enacting the French border defence of the Maginot Line without being sent to a muddy swamp in Belgium for six weeks.

Festivals have changed dramatically since then. Nowadays, the tents are sponsored (as well as some of the bands), there are mobile-phone charging stations and the hospitality areas are so lavish that you feel short-changed if your cocaine is not delivered on a silver platter atop a dwarf's head.

I can actually remember my first festival experience. Upon arrival, I treated it as a vast musical library as I fretfully rushed from stage to stage, lest I missed a particularly invigorating performance by some hapless Congolese drum combo. Ah, the innocent folly of youth!

Then a friend gave me a tab of acid and I spent the next two days in a cardboard box talking Esperanto with red-faced goblins while drawing William Morris shapes with a wand fashioned out of woad and elm. It was like discovering the map to Atlantis, or perhaps, more pertinently, the definition of self-debasement (wet wipes had yet to be invented).

What often deters the weaker of will and lily of liver is the discomfort. "I like my luxury," they say, as though we like nothing better than contracting typhus while listening to shit indie bands in the middle of a monsoon. They miss the point. Festivals are not about the bands and the acts and the line-ups – why else would Glastonbury sell out before the names have been announced? They are a kind of super-community. They are mini-cities. They are the Imagined Perfection of a Golden Age That Never Was. Or a big care in the community party with better music and worse drugs. Is there another place in the world, for example, where every street is populated with ruddy-faced loons wearing primary-coloured jester's hats, shouting, "Es! Trips! Weed!" as though selling evening newspapers?

Nobody likes discomfort. Least of all someone who understands the warming qualities of a chunky-knit Aran sweater or a night at the Waldorf Astoria. But it is precisely the adverse weather – the typhoon conditions, the incessant rain, the snow lashing down on your badly holed igloo – that knits these wonderful temporary communities together. And, of course, ketamine.

Let's face it, when the rain comes, what you need is not an umbrella and wellies (although clearly they do help), but some good friends and, even better K. It will, admittedly, not keep you dry or prevent you from contracting trench foot. But thanks to its immense dissociative powers, it allows you to welcome mud into your life as though greeting a long-lost friend. Food becomes a mere frippery, along with consciousness and limbs. Don't forget, it's been used on amputees in Vietnam and as a horse tranquilliser. I have a simple motto: if it's good enough for Red Rum, it's good enough for me.

This year we took our toddler daughter to Glastonbury. "Are you mad?" asked friends. It gave the festival experience a new edge, a new sense of danger and, thanks to the mud, new ways in which to lose wellington boots. We only mislaid her three times (and only once deliberately). She loved it, though. She's already asking when we are next going "tenting". And the music? Who cares. We had the most fun it's possible to have while living like rutting hippopotamuses.

RULES
Do not wash. Only poltroons, popinjays and pomade addicts wash during a festival. This is why wet wipes were invented.
Do not eat. Eat well before you arrive. If you feel hungry at a festival, take more amphetamines.
Don't take a capsule wardrobe. Take the clothes in which you usually decorate and a spare pair of knickers (in case of incontinent episodes).
Always wear a sign around your neck saying: "I am the lord and your saviour, the ruler of all Narnia. If lost, please deliver to…" (in case of psychotic episodes).

Glastonbury Festival 2007 Matt Cardy/Getty Images

Members of royalty and festival-goers with ideas above their station insist on wearing Hunter wellies. The rest should be content with two Tesco bags over a pair of badly worn Converse trainers.❖

3

Drugs

‘ I've never had a problem with drugs.
I've had problems with the police ’

Keith Richards

Caned and Able –
a Sensible Guide to Gear
By Howard Marks

Howard, the author of Mr Nice, is a not very sensible man

DON'T DRINK AND DRIVE. Smoke and fly. And when out shopping, try before you buy. Test hashish by sucking a piece. A peppery taste is good. Press a small piece in your hand. The quicker it darkens and softens, the better. Burn a piece: the rate at which it burns is determined by the ratio of resin to plant matter. Fluffy, spongy, gritty or dirty shit is predominantly plant matter and burns jerkily with a brownish-black, nasty-smelling smoke. Denser, purer hashish burns slowly and completely, giving off a milky-white smoke with a spicy aroma. Test marijuana under a magnifying glass: look for a thick coating of white or golden crystals and stalked glands topped with resin. Ensure the weed is not musty and mouldy or dry and dusty when broken and rolled. (Hashish versus marijuana? Mainly a question of taste.)

Some clowns smoke without tobacco. They're off the planet (but think they're saving it). The use of tobacco ensures the mixture burns at the right temperature and enhances the high with nicotine, one very poorly understood drug. Original tobacco (*Nicotiana rustica*) is a hallucinogen and immeasurably more potent than tobacco generally available today (*Nicotiana tabacum*). French idiot Jean Nicot (from whom the word "nicotine" is derived) imported a few tons into France but brought back the wrong stuff: *tabacum* rather than *rustica*. There was just enough nicotine in the tobacco to get addicted but not to get nutted, so everyone got hooked without getting stoned.

And so to spliffs. Although king-size papers indicate, without doubt, that you are a stoner, they thankfully require none of the tedious origami skills of the master craftsman who will bore you shitless rolling spliffs in the shape of boats, planes, cones, tulips, swallows' tails and

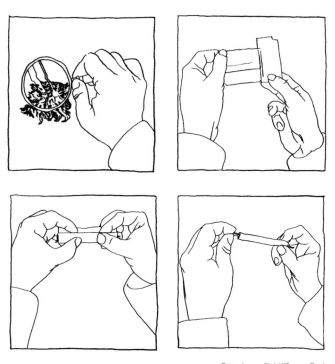

Peter James Field/ZeegenRush

other zoological bits. One simple, non-artistic method of skinning up normal rolling papers is as follows: take two papers, overlap them lengthways by about 1.5cm, moisten the gum where they overlap and stick together to form one new double-width skin. Take a third skin and lick right along the gum. Stick this third skin along either of the two sides of the double-width skin that lie at right angles to its gummed edge, and there you have a king-size skin. If rolling in darkness or when completely wrecked, green-packeted Rizlas are useful, because the corners along the non-sticky edge are cut off, making them easier to identify.

The smoking mixture will be the crushed leaves of the marijuana plant or heated and crumbled resin (or both), consistently mingled with very high nicotine-content tobacco. Uniformly distribute this mixture along the length of the skin, which has its gummed edge facing upwards and towards you. With thumbs, forefingers and middle fingers, roll the skin into a tight-fitting tube around the smoking mixture. Lick the gummed edge. Twist one end of the cylinder. In the other end, insert a small, rolled-up piece of cardboard. Light up the twisted end.

Etiquette requires one to pass the joint in a circular fashion among those present. Nobody is forced to smoke the joint, but each is expected to pass it on. "Bogarting" (hoarding the joint) is a serious breach of protocol. People too stoned to smoke the spliff, let alone pass it on, are expected to be skipped over, and a joint can be courteously removed from someone who does not seem to be sharing the consensus of reality.

If you are with someone you fancy, share a "powerhit", "blowback" or "nice one". Carefully surround the burning end of the joint with his or her mouth and take a hit from the other end. If that doesn't get you off your tits and you are still anxious to determine just how much THC the human body can consume and still function on a basic level, try a bong, ideally a large glass one, hand-blown in south Germany and filled with ice to cool the smoke. THC can shit-face you more than any drug. There's no real technique: just bung in as much weed as you can and suck like a Hoover. Try not to breathe any oxygen, just smoke, for several minutes. The bridge of your nose will throb as the cannabinols rape and pillage your memory cells. Butterflies will puke in your guts. You will lose the power of speech as your balls and dick shrivel and freeze. Shagging will be like wanking in ice-cold water. But you'll recover and want another hit.

Thank you for smoking. ❖

Cook with Cannabis Without OD-ing Your Guests

By Tim Pilcher

Tim, as the author of The Cannabis Cookbook, is a man who knows. His culinary low was knocking out a dinner party for 12 hours with his hash brownies

"TASTE THE HASHISH, guest of mine. Taste the hashish!" – Alexander Dumas, The Count of Monte Cristo, 1844

In these puritanical times, smoking is getting a pretty bum rap. Now banned in all manner of public places, the cannabis smoker has it twice as tough – no longer can you hope that through the haze, your cheeky spliff might be considered an innocent rollie.

> **The best rule of thumb is the size of your guests. Of course it's not always possible to weigh everyone beforehand (and you may cause offence)**

So how's a stoner supposed to partake of the sacred herb? Through gastronomic ganja genius, of course. It spares your lungs and, combined with fine food, it simply doubles the pleasure. Every single part of the cannabis plant is edible, from the leaves and buds to the seeds and even the stalks, and it can be prepared in endless ways, from eating it raw in a salad (you can pass it off as oregano to Grandma) to sprinkling in casseroles or grinding down the seeds to make hemp flour for pasta and bread.

Cooking with cannabis is not an exact science. No single recipe will suit everyone, and a little trial and error is required to find out the ideal quantities for you and your dinner guests. Err on the side of caution – it's hard to see exactly where the edge lies, and if you fall off, you might land in either a blissful (but not very useful) deep sleep or find yourself befriending the toilet bowl. The best rule of thumb is the size of your guests. Of course, it's not always possible to weigh everyone beforehand (and you may cause offence), but here's a rough guide:

Weight	Amount of cannabis bud (per person, per meal)
Under 57kg (9 stone):	¼ - ⅓ tsp
57kg-83kg (9-13 stone):	½ - ⅔ tsp
83kg-102kg (13-16 stone):	⅔ -1 tsp
102kg-128kg (16-20 stone):	1-1½ tsp
134kg + (21 stone +):	1½-2 level tsp

The connoisseur knows that eating cannabis is a completely different beast to smoking it. Smoking delivers a near-instant rush. The peak high from eating the plant might hit as much as two hours later. The effect is also intensified, more trippy and lasts a lot longer – anything up to five to six hours – which makes it the perfect dinner-party catalyst when nobody has to rush off straight away (but go easy on second helpings).

Now, you can just sprinkle grass into a stew, but to get *really* wasted on tetrahydrocannabinol (THC, the psychoactive ingredient), it needs to be extracted from the seeds, buds or leaves. The sticky buds contain the highest levels of THC and the leaves the least. THC is only soluble in oils, fats and butter (and alcohol, but that's for another time) – it won't break down in water on its own. The best thing is to have a constant supply of cannabutter to hand. This can be used in just about every recipe to replace regular butter or cooking oil. Here's how to make it:

Cannabutter

Ingredients
500g (1lb) of butter or ghee (clarified butter)
50g (2oz) of finely ground/powdered cannabis

Method
1. Melt the butter or ghee in a saucepan. Add the marijuana. Simmer on a low heat and stir for a few minutes until the butter turns a greenish colour.
2. Strain the butter through a very fine sieve and keep the remaining leafy material for later use.
3. To crank up the wow factor, repeat step one by adding more fresh marijuana to the same butter.

Rick Morris Pushinsky

Cannabutter can be frozen or kept for a long time in the refrigerator (cover in chilled water to prevent air getting to it). The leftover leafy material can be transformed into a tasty, powerful drink by simmering it in hot milk or vodka sweetened with honey – et voilà, an Indian bhang.

Cooking cannabis increases its potency by activating the THC, but overcooking can destroy it, so always slightly undercook. As with all cooking ingredients, you get what you pay for (low-grade hashish, or "soap bar", can contain anything from engine oil to shit). Try and find a reliable organic grower. Better still, grow your own alongside your rosemary, thyme and basil. It's a hardy plant and very easy to cultivate – it is a weed, after all (you can order seeds legally off the internet). Now get in the kitchen and pop that pot in your pans.❖

How to Score Drugs Abroad (and I don't mean Ibiza)

By Martin Deeson

Martin spent years travelling abroad for Loaded magazine,
but claims that if you can remember Bogota, then you
weren't there

SCORING DRUGS ABROAD is by far the best way to immerse
yourself in a foreign culture. There are few better ways to discover the
true face of your destination than staggering around the backstreets of
a city enquiring, "Où est la cocayeen?" or, indeed, miming the action of
smoking a spliff.

The rules go as follows:

1. Taxi drivers and tuk-tuk operators are your first port of call
In many parts of the world, minicab drivers are drug dealers. In Rio, for
instance, they keep the contraband under the seats or, in a couple of
strange cases, behind the headlights. Failing that, the people whose job
it is to ferry you around a city late at night are, if you think about it, the
most likely to know where late-night activities can be found. Prostitutes,
narcotics and rent-by-the-hour love motels are the bread and butter of
the minicab driver, so stick up your hand and hail yourself a short cut to
the low life.

2. Make like Marcel Marceau and learn to mime
Not knowing the words for "spiff", "gear" or "where can I buy?" should
not be an obstacle to the international traveller. It is amazing how well
one can do by merely acting out the ritual of taking one's drug of
choice. If in doubt, just think what one of the younger royals might do
if presented with a card saying "Scarface" during a game of charades
on Christmas Day in Buck Pal.

Yulee Hong

3. Go low to get high

A common mistake of those wanting to get high abroad is to head for the foreign equivalent of Soho House. You just have to think these things through. Can you imagine how you would be received there, speaking only Spanish and demanding, "Is it possible you are knowing where I may sniff some Coca-Cola?" Now imagine how you would be treated in a Soho alley if you mimed snorting a line and then rubbed your thumb and forefinger together in the internationally accepted sign language for hard cash. They would be queuing to serve you.

4. To get happy, go gay

To lonely travellers in distant lands who wish to get off their nuts, there is one place you are guaranteed drugs of the highest quality in a safe environment: from the fat woman by the loos in a gay club. For many years, my job as a travel journalist meant I would find myself parachuted into a strange city, jet-lagged, disorientated and in need of a spliff or a pill or a wrap. After a while, I developed a failsafe method of achieving this without trawling the backstreets: ask a cab driver for the nearest gay club and, once there, proceed to the loos. I have seldom been disappointed. Gay men demand the best – the pink pound is only spent on top-notch product.

5. When scoring drugs off prostitutes, do not give cash in advance

Whores will, of course, sell anything – but they will also try and rip you off. On one occasion, I gave a streetwalker in Sydney $100 to score me a bag of weed. She gave me her trainers as a deposit, and then nipped through the door of an apartment block to get the cure I needed for my jet lag. Twenty minutes later and she hadn't returned, so I tried the door of said apartment block, only to find that beyond said door was just a building site. All that remained was a 2ft-thick façade of a building, left abandoned after the wrecker's ball had demolished the rest of it. It was a front, like a film studio lot, and as I looked through the open front door onto a field of rubble, I realised she had long run. And her trainers didn't fit me.

6. If all else fails, go to the chemist

If you really can't get your hands on anything, and you are the kind of person who just can't live with yourself unmedicated, then head for the farmacia. Look for side effects that include "May cause drowsiness" or "May cause anxiety". One pill will make you bigger and one will make you smaller. It's just up to you to work out which way you want to go. Now who says travel doesn't broaden the mind? ❖

A Field Guide to Magic Mushrooms

By Patrick Harding

Author of Mushroom Hunting, Patrick is a 1960s
survivor (despite inhaling) who now prefers his
mushrooms in a good risotto

I'M OLD ENOUGH to know that Jefferson Airplane is no competition for easyJet. The band's lead singer Grace Slick sang about Alice eating a mushroom – not as part of a calorie-free diet, though it did make her smaller than a size zero. Alice first experienced Wonderland in 1865: on meeting a hookah-smoking caterpillar, she learnt that consumption of one side of his mushroom made her grow taller, the other offered diminishing returns. As an ageing mushroom-lover, I set out to discover from whom Charles Dodgson (aka Lewis Carroll) had received his mycological wisdom.

Checking my bookcase, A Plain and Easy Account of British Fungi, by MC Cooke (published in 1862), caught my eye. Under fly agaric, which has a large, scarlet cap studded with white spots, surely everyone's idea of a magic mushroom, Cooke wrote: "In Siberia, it supplies the inhabitants with the means of intoxication…" Ingestion causes "Erroneous impressions of size and distance… a straw lying in the road becomes a formidable object." My quest was complete.

Nineteenth-century Russians dried their "magics". Just Google "magic mushroom" for offers of heat-dried fly agaric (*Amanita muscaria*), where the chemical structure of the poisons has been changed into a safe, psychoactive compound. Stick to dried cap material – fresh can produce unpleasant symptoms, but despite accounts to the contrary, fly agaric is not deadly poisonous. Between 10 and 20g of dried mushroom will result in a trip (induced by the chemical muscimol) that lasts up to 12 hours. In most countries, consumption is quite legal – it grows in America, much of Europe and New Zealand.

So you thought Father Christmas (think flying over houses, red and white suit, ho, ho, ho) was based on St Nicholas? In Lapland, reindeer-

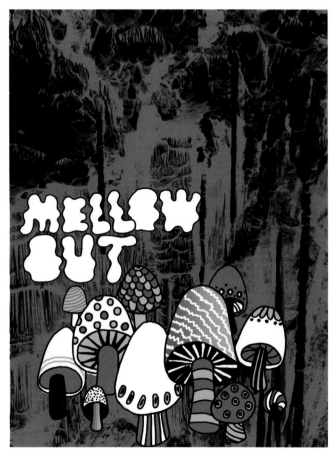

Travis Stearns/iammintcondition.com

herding tribes have a long history of fly agaric usage – no wonder Santa was so happy. Baden-Powell's Scouting and Guiding youth movement is not without its magic mushroom; my daughter "flew up" from Brownies to Guides by jumping a plastic fly agaric. The first Scout camps were held on Brownsea Island, where I was delighted to find hundreds of real fly agaric mushrooms nestling beneath birch trees, their typical habitat.

A fly agaric trip is far from predictable, so many would-be flyers opt for smaller magic mushrooms, species of *Psilocybe* (the p is silent). In 1957, Gordon Wasson's article in *Life* magazine about the traditional use of hallucinogenic mushrooms in Central America kick-started 1960s counterculture in the USA. *Psilocybe mexicana* is the most infamous American species containing the psychoactive drugs psilocin and psilocybin, the possession of which is now illegal in the States.

Modern Britain was slow to embrace *Psilocybe*, not helped by the antagonism of journalists more dependent on alcohol. A 1970s British biology textbook expressed surprise that the common liberty cap (*Psilocybe semilanceata*) had never been used as a casual inebriant. Undergraduates read the book, visiting American students helped and the craze for magic mushrooms took off.

Fruiting in large numbers among grassland, especially unimproved upland grassland, and also in playing fields and parks from late summer to autumn, the liberty cap is a "little brown job" with a date-brown, nipple-topped cap (little fingernail-sized), drying pale tan with dark gills and a wiggly, matchstick-sized stem. (Beware poisonous lookalikes; consult a mushroom guidebook before harvesting.)

Try 25 mushrooms (cap and stem) – honey masks the taste. Effects begin within 20 minutes and last up to four hours. I enjoyed the visual hallucinations and also found that everything suddenly had an aroma. Sense of touch becomes more sensitised, which magnifies sexual experience, itself further enhanced by a time-slowing sensation. Don't mix with alcohol or take when really down, do take with friends and be prepared for flashbacks, typically in Monday morning's rush hour.

Trade in dried magics is brisk as they keep for years, though, unfortunately, with some loss of potency. The law remained a grey area in Britain until a relaxation in the early Noughties resulted in a "mushrooming" of websites and Amsterdam-style shroom shops. In a typical panic reaction to people enjoying themselves tax-free, the law was changed in 2005. This outlawed grow-your-own kits and dried mushrooms, and even threatened landowners where the fungi grew. The recent fashion of spreading wood chippings on council rose beds, paths and children's play areas, however, encourages the spread of the psychoactive blueleg brownie (*Psilocybe cyanescens*). So if you're taking the kids to play, you could still arrive in Wonderland (albeit illegally). Happy landings.❖

An Homage to Pillage

By James Delingpole

James is a journalist and author. Now that he is older and wiser, he has exchanged drugs for writing thrilling, funny novels set in the second world war, including Coward on the Beach. All thanks to MDMA, without which he might have ended up a lawyer

OBVIOUSLY, I DON'T take drugs any more. They're bad, they're illegal and they promulgate crime and moral decadence. But suppose one of my little ones was to ask sweetly: "Daddy, I'd like to experiment with proscribed substances. Are there any in particular that you'd recommend?" I'd be ducking my duty as a parent if I didn't give them a straight answer. "Darling," I'd say. "If you're going to do one drug and one drug only, let it be Ecstasy."

Now I feel a little outré saying this, because I know there are lots of smackheads out there who'll insist you can't beat heroin. And I realise that crack gives a much better, more instantaneous high, that mushrooms are more organic, that LSDs are more adventurous, and that for general-purpose, all-round manageable, reality-suppressing life-enhancement, there's nothing to equal good old-fashioned non-skunk grass.

But for me, E covers the most bases. All drugs are a trade-off in one way or another. In return for the gorgeous numbness of heroin, you must pay a price including vomit, several hours as a drooling vegetable and the possibility of lifelong addiction. When you do cocaine, you accept that not only are you going to be transformed into a complete wanker, but that in about 20 minutes, you'll need to do another line, then another, then another, each one with diminishing returns.

So it goes on. Crack? Too addictive and with terrible lows. Acid? Too scary and demanding. Dope? Too mood-dependent. The depressing truth is – future Shulgins please note and get on the case ASAP – the dream drug, which doesn't have some kind of downside, has yet to be invented. So the best we can do, for the moment, is plump for the least worst option.

And as least worst options go, my, what a marvellous little fellow Ecstasy is. Let's first examine its upsides: puts huge gurning smile on your face; makes you want to shag everyone and, better still, makes everyone who's on the drug want to shag you; enables you to dance, dance, dance way past your bedtime; makes you understand repetitive beats in a way you never quite did before; makes you realise just how amazingly special and lovely – no, I mean really, REALLY lovely – your friends are; helps you to form undying friendships with complete strangers; gives you really great, ultra-sensuous sex that goes on and on; enhances your sensory perceptions generally so that pretty things (flowers; some amazingly shiny, 3D-effect thingy someone shows you on the dancefloor, though you're too monged to work out what it is) and nice textures (velvet; the back of a gorgeous girl's neck) become almost unbearably exquisite; makes you realise what ought to be obvious, but so very often isn't – that it is better to be happy than unhappy.

Now let's examine the downsides: can make it quite hard to achieve orgasm; makes you look a bit of a fool to people who aren't on the drug; can lead to mild jaw-ache; gives you Wednesday blues; can, if you react adversely or drink too much water, lead to sudden, ugly death.

Note how very different in length the two lists are. I rest my case. Oh, all right. You'll accuse me of cheating a bit, and I have. I could have made the downsides list much longer by adding things like, "Makes you so pathetically desperate three or four days afterwards that you attempt to recapture that moment with long, reminiscing phone calls to the people who were there with you." Then again, is that such a bad thing? And okay, okay, I haven't dealt with the danger side, notably the risk of death. But we're not going there for two reasons. One, this is a hedonist's guide, not the hair-shirt, moralising prohibitionist's version. Two, you could construct a similar argument about everything from peanuts to cars to bungee-jumping to beehives, and if you were to ban everything that was dangerous, where would you stop?

If I'm honest, I can't say I'm overjoyed at the prospect that one day my kids will be as mashed and off their faces as I was when I took my first pill in the late 1980s. But I shan't try to stop them. They will probably make fools of themselves by snogging strangers and vowing undying friendship to people who, in the cold light of reality, aren't quite as interesting as they seemed on MDMA. Still, I can think of worse ways of frittering away one's youth.❖

Psychoactivity in the Strangest Places

By Howard Marks

Howard is a drugs war veteran and the author of Mr Nice.
He is used to thinking laterally when it comes to drugs

WE UNDERSTAND THERE is a war against drugs. Most drugs are
plants. Presumably, there is not a civil war within the plant kingdom.
Accordingly, a section of the animal kingdom (probably people) must
have declared war against a section of the plant kingdom. How would
we survive if the plants won?

If plants ruled the world, they wouldn't want us eating, smoking and
snorting them. Vegetarians would probably be executed. We would have
to survive on meat. And what about getting wankered?

Worry not. For your daily beverage, drink reindeer piss. Arctic Circle
reindeer eat magic mushrooms and go into psychedelic trances. Their
piss gets you off your tits. The Chuckchi people of eastern Siberia are
rarely without a couple of bags of reindeer piss by their side. At least
once a week, eat some giraffe. The Humr tribe of Baggara arabs, who
live in Kordofan, Sudan, are normally strict abstainers. But they kill
giraffes and boil up their livers and bone marrow to make a mind-
bending hallucinatory drink called *umm nyolokh.*

Some insects, including ground-up scarab beetles, ants and
tarantulas, get you spannered. Some make you want to shag all night.
Try Spanish fly, made from beetles' wings. "If anointed on the soles of
the feet, testicles and perineum, it provokes and stirs up lust to a
miracle in both sexes and invigorates the feeble instruments of
generation," as the English physician William Salmon discovered in
1693. It's not a patch on Viagra, but it does cause itching on the genitals
that is excellent fun to scratch. Catch some South American birds called
pitohui and eat them. You'll see heavenly visions of birds of paradise.
Extract the venom from a load of cobras (kings and all), crystallize it,

Martin Harvey/Getty Images

put it in a pipe and smoke it. Hear the music of snake charmers. Gather newts, salamanders, frogs and toads. Witches, when they're not poaching cats' brains in bats' blood, suck toads until their warts pop and the pus dribbles out. The pus is then smeared on a broomstick and rammed up the vagina to give the feeling of flying.

Every ancient civilisation whose culture incorporated psychoactive drugs has ended up on a diet of fish. Not all fish works, just shellfish (especially oysters) and a few white fish, which have to be either smoked first or coddled in one's mother's milk. Haddock is the best. The standard explanation is that bits of fish replace the natural serotonin that psychoactive drugs deplete.

Fish junkies eat Japanese blowfish, or *fugu*. The ovaries, roe, liver, gonads, intestines and skin all contain the lethal toxin tetrodotoxin, a tiny drop of which guarantees paralysis. Ten minutes after ingestion, the tongue tingles and twitches and the mouth itches. Vomiting, drooling, dizziness, feelings of doom and convulsions quickly follow, giving way to respiratory failure, then death. There is no known antidote. The chef's goal is not to eliminate the poison, but rather to preserve an amount small enough to provide that special *fugu* tingling, numbness and euphoria without killing the diner. Rational people don't dice with death to eat a hundred quid's worth of fish for its taste. They do so to get high. At the very heart of the word "intoxication" is the word "toxic". If the shit can kill you, it can get you high.

Voodoo sorcerers create zombies with the poison *coupe poudre,* which causes that death-like trance state. The active ingredient is our friend tetrodotoxin (some newts and salamanders also possess this poison). A zombie is not a revived dead person, but a living person brain-damaged by a near-fatal dose of tetrodotoxin.

Drink some spunk. In the past, it was believed that women became pregnant through all kinds of weird shite, for example, fire, wind, star formations and even the Holy Ghost. Guys didn't think spunk was for reproduction, they just loved to drink the stuff, even if it was smelly, stale or someone else's. Incubi (devil's gofers) stole spunk while guys were having wet dreams and made cocktails out of it to get bladdered. Spunk was viewed as what kept men kicking, so wanking and shagging were frowned upon. Losing it was not cool, but one could always reach for the spunk nightcap.

We need not fear the day of the triffids.❖

Life through the K Hole

By Charlie Norton

In 1996, a vet friend raided his lab and gave Charlie, a journalist, some white powder. He nearly drowned in the River Cam and happily floated to the surface. It was ketamine. He knows to stay away from rivers now

"OH, YOU NAUGHTY BOY. What are you doing out here? Is that coke?"

"No, it's psychedelic heroin. In 10 minutes, I'll be floating above the main course and, though I may not know my name, it will make sitting at this fucking dinner party talking about house prices somewhat tolerable."

"You are silly."

"Well, quite."

When people hear the word ketamine they tsk and say that they don't want to take horse tranquilliser, or that they "know" it's some kind of dirty gay drug. Others end up angst-ridden and unable to move after snorting a fat line of K like it's charlie. But take it semi-professionally, with just a snitch of the "cat valium" on a house key, ideally when you have just come up on a pill, then you can ride a waking dream into another world. As Jay Stevens said in Storming Heaven: LSD and the American Dream: "If MDMA got into third gear, then K was in tenth."

It's not like I'm ploughing a chemical blade through my cortex all on my own. In 2006, 30% of clubbers used K. It's dirt cheap for its damage and longevity (£15-£30 a gram), far less addictive than nicotine, not a bad comedown after a pure session and is outlawed at class-C level, along with weed. It's the drugs trend of the decade.

If Timothy Leary was the acid guru of the 1960s, then the Kiwi Dr Karl Jansen is the king of K today. According to Dr K (as he is known) in his book, Ketamine: Dreams and Realities, the K hole is a place reached after "a dose sufficient to make coherent communication impossible" – when you find yourself in an incredibly detailed world deep behind your curtain for half an hour. Approaching the hole, a conversation might be: "I can see behind that plant... My name is... Christ, I'm high, so high... ha, heh, heh, what did I say? I'm a mad, mad avenging demon..."

When you first come up (after 10-30 minutes), you start to feel very floaty, you walk like Bambi and, with the spatial side of your brain opened up, you enter a Matrix-like world. Even the most mundane scenery takes on a magical hue – nature is more defined and your eye can spy all the geometry in the world. Now is not the time to operate heavy machinery (the usual), go wine-tasting (booze with K = sickness), play Scrabble or fuss that you've lost the rest of the K in your pocket – it will be there somewhere. Do skip in a field, play mischievous gags and act out slow-motion mime sequences.

Sometimes, it's best not to think too much on K (easier said than done), but your whizzing mind will work out the most fascinating thread of thought and leave you blank when you try and open your mouth. If you are a tortured wreck in life, however, you will be more tortured on the other side. It can be psychologically addictive, and it's easy to think you've been chosen for a higher purpose when on special K, which means you have to be careful not to look for omens and portents in everyday life.

It can be feeling or unfeeling, turning you into a circus performer or a curious scientist. Sexually, it can produce the most sordidly orgasmic sex or it can feel like you are being licked by some kind of lizard – which will still seem fascinating.

If you're lucky, you might get a Near Death Experience (NDE) when you travel towards a light with the wind in your hair, heading to oblivion with nothing before you to register where you are. There are K meccas, or "blacKholes": for example, in Vauxhall, London, the club Fire is where the world points down to the earth's core and the light show offers a tunnel towards an NDE. But for the partying ketanaut, there is nothing better than a pilgrimage to Ibiza's apocalyptic DC10 Club. Score your K off the guy in the wheelchair (really) and approach the centre of the amphitheatre, where you'll get drawn towards the pulsing throng thrashing to hard house like a mass of armoured insects in tune to the beat and order of the Queen of K. But you can be just as happy alone in a verdant glade or deep in a plush, red chaise longue. And there's a happy ending: Dr K says limited experience of NDEs can lead to more altruism and less neurosis. You don't get that on coke.❖

Drugs: a Doctor's Honest View

By Dr Chloe Britten

Dr Britten has spent countless Saturday nights in Accident & Emergency (mainly working)

Oliver Wright/digitoli.com

Cannabis Active ingredient THC targets the brain's cannabinoid receptors (ie we were made for it). Prognosis: acts in minutes (or 1-2 hours if ingested); lasts 1-4 hours. Subject presents with non-aggressive euphoria, rambling but "hilarious" stories and emmental-head amnesia. Long-term risks include carcinogenicity, exacerbation of underlying mental illness, reduced sperm count and gynaecomastia (man boobs). Legality: Class C (official warning for possession). Avoid urine drug test for 3-5 days (12 weeks if chronic user).

Amphetamines Synthetic forms of adrenalin, acting as physical and mental stimulants; potency varies from amphetamine sulphate (speed) to highly addictive crystal meth. Prognosis: hits in minutes; tails off after 3-

8 hours. Subject presents with eyes on stalks, jaw-grinding, inability to stop moving and complete disinterest in sleeping, hospital-vending machines and shutting the fuck up; the subdued comedown includes a penis the size of a peanut. Excessive use leads to paranoia, psychosis and the need for a good orthodontist to fix teeth stumps. Legality: Class B (offence to possess unless prescribed). Avoid urine tests for 72 hours.

Ecstasy Synthetic, mildly hallucinogenic stimulant (active ingredient is MDMA); taken orally, it increases the amount of feelgood hormones dopamine and serotonin. Prognosis: acts in 30-60 minutes; lasts 4-6 hours. Subject presents keenness to hug attending doctor and inclination to dance to bleeping pagers. Comedown sees patient tired and emotional due to temporary serotonin imbalance (salved by tryptophan-rich chocolate, turkey and bananas). Risks include dancing-induced hyperthermia and overhydration (basically, you drink too much water, your brain swells, you fit, you die). Legality: Class A (illegal to have, sell or give away). Not routinely checked in urine tests, though often tests positive for amphetamines.

Amyl Nitrite (or poppers) Sniffed from the bottle, causes dilation of blood vessels giving short-lived head rush then short-lived headache. Also promotes anal relaxation, if so desired. Possession not illegal and is often sold as "room aroma" in sex shops.

Ketamine An anaesthetic (snorted or swallowed) that inhibits neural pathways causing body/mind dissociation. Prognosis: acts in minutes; lasts 2-3 hours. Initially stimulates, then subjects experience paralysing psychedelia as they plunge towards the "K hole", a near-comatose state which can be life-changingly insightful or just plain scary; patients present nonsensical, zombified mutterings. Its paralysing properties make it hard to continue self-administrating to fatal doses. Legality: Class C. Not routinely screened.

LSD Synthetic psychedelic derived from ergot fungus, usually soaked into tabs of paper. Prognosis: acts in 20 minutes–2 hours; wears off after 8-12 hours, with trippy flashbacks days or weeks later, if lucky. Subject presents euphoria, increased sensory awareness, near-religious flashes of enlightenment and hallucinations not unlike a Beatles album cover. Amplifies current mood – neurotics likely to have worse trips. Contrary to the weirdy-beardy stereotype, LSD isn't known to cause long-term psychiatric problems, unless existing history. Legality: Class A. Not routinely tested, though detectable in urine for 48 hours, and commenting on chattering needles may arouse suspicion.

Magic mushrooms Naturally occurring psychedelic, non-toxic fungi. Similar effects to LSD but shorter-lived; mixing with Ecstasy ("candy-flipping") can reduce chance of a bad trip. Main risk is "mushtaken" identity – illness/death from eating a poisonous variety (see A Field Guide to Magic Mushrooms, page 77). Legality: Class A. Not part of routine drug testing.

Cocaine Stimulates nervous and cardiovascular systems through release of dopamine; processed with sodium bicarbonate, it forms crack cocaine, a smokable, shorter-acting but more intense – and highly addictive – hit. Prognosis: fast-acting (minutes) and short-lived (30 minutes). Giveaway signs: mucky nostrils, more frequent loo trips than a bad case of cystitis, jaw-grinding, dilated pupils, a fine line between sparkling conversationalist and egocentric bore. Comedown: big sulks due to diminished dopamine. Risks include respiratory and cardiac problems, and nasal septum destruction – nose down for the camera, now. Legality: Class A. Avoid urine test for 72 hours; detectable in hair for 90 days.

Opiates Family of addictive painkilling drugs that trigger opiate receptors to mimic endorphins; includes over-the-counter codeine, methadone (used and abused in management of opioid dependence), morphine and heroin. Heroin prognosis: smoked or injected, an instant, intense rush followed by sense of wellbeing so great that not even the grimmest side effects matter (nausea, inhaling one's own vomit, constipation, itching, difficulty getting it up, overdose, death; it is, however, good for coughs). Hardcore use with cocaine ("speedballing"), whereby both drugs potentiate each other, sometimes to unmanageable highs, as John Belushi and River Phoenix should have been warned. Legality: Class A. Avoid urine test for 48 hours; worth remembering codeine can give false positives.❖

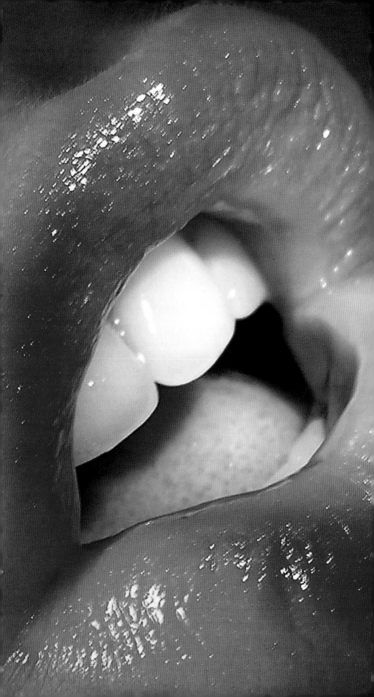

4

Sex

❝ Life is a sexually
transmitted disease ❞

RD Laing

First Base: On the Pull

By Tom Stubbs

Tom, a writer and stylist, is technically neutral and acts as special envoy to both sexes on this matter

ODD FORCES ARE at play in the pulling equation, many indeterminable, some almost mystical. Some factors are sacrosanct manlore, others are unfounded speculation. Rules exist, but nothing is black and white in this game. And it is a game. Not like cricket or football, but a game of sexy chess. It's by no means easy. Broadcast on-the-pull signals, and spend the night alone. Clubs and pubs are rammed full of people who are after some, but being seen to be sniffing about is no aphrodisiac. Same sketch with rubber johnnies: if you carry them with intent, your presumption seeps out, and you'll get naught. Have an empty-out before you leave the house. Assume you'll not be serving tonight. A pal used to sit down and agree a schedule for the evening, for example, "Tonight, only snogging. Nothing more." Making solemn agreements to this effect would somehow work as girl catnip.

The Mass Market The Bitch Dredger was a chap who'd go anywhere and pull something from the darkest depths. He worked on a spread-betting system. In any given venue, there's always a handful of girls that are either a) available for dalliances or b) interested in you. You just have to hedge your bets without looking keen. In the numbers-based approach, get your head round knock-backs. You don't even really need to do the groundwork. If, say, one out of 10 lasses is potentially game, all you have to do is nonchalantly get clocked by the whole gaff at some point and monitor if anybody is interested. Let them do the work while you scan for signs of attention.

Fall in Love / Mio Matsumoto

Don't Care About Stuff Not giving a hoot is a good thing. Ladies want in if you're not bothered. Fact. They question why you're so comfortable. Maybe because you're a perpetual laugh and guaranteed good company. Mooning about in the shadows is a low-frequency operation, and quite liable to turn up a zero result.

Chat-up Squads of mugs are delivering rehearsed lines to women. Lines are rubbish. Pre-meditated banter doesn't make you look like a relaxed fella who gets plenty. Instead, act normal and lark about. Girls are frequently bored, and get excited when someone might relieve this. Acting up and being gregarious will land you in conversations. Even if the chat is not going well, stay buoyant. Other interested parties may be observing your progress and admiring the way that you handle abuse. Laughing and talking are key. Once a keen potential recipient is locked on, keep your head cool and the "No sexy business is about to happen" mantra on a loop in your head.

Target Pulling The next type of scenario is the target persuasion. Identify someone as particularly fanciable and then aim to ensnare her. Nonchalance and a healthy dose of humour are going to help. At a drinks do or dinner party, agree with aspects of the target's conversation, disagree with others. It shows you have balls and opinion. If she likes you, she won't mind. A frisson of friction might excite things. Again, get it firmly in your head that zilch is gonna happen.

The Long-Term Project A fondness for someone can make things hard. Evenings when you stand down, go home alone or even opt out of paying her attention might all be part of the groundwork. Research is useful. Find out what she's into: music, scenes, films etc. Have opinions on these, and make them engaging. Don't over-egg the pudding and appear stalkerish. Do move the focus of conversation around: about her, a note on your feelings, another reference, back to her.

And if none of this works, don't beat yourself up – or me, for that matter. Perhaps there's a still-warm old relationship dumping baggage at her feet and causing cross-referenced reasoning. Certainly, there are always pheromones and cycles, spite shags and self-loathing, plus moods, chemistry and scenarios. It's a proper lottery. Best just get out and enjoy it. One last tip: once on a roll, stay on it for as long as possible. Drag it out for a lifetime, if you can. There's nothing like getting loads to access you loads more.❖

How to Visit a Lap Dancing Club
(Without Losing All Your Money or Self Respect)

By Martin Deeson

Martin has never managed either

"BOYS," DAVID BOWIE sang, "Heaven loves ya/ The clouds part for ya/ Nothing stands in your way/ When you're a boy."

Dave was right – it used to be great to be a boy, but sadly, the days of the Rat Pack are long gone. Who can blame us if the modern male hankers occasionally for a simpler era, when he could click his fingers, Dean Martin-style, at a comely cocktail waitress and say: "Hello, darling! Can I have two martinis, and why don't you come here and put those puppies in my face while you're at it?"

Now, us men are confused, tired and overworked. After a hard week sucking the corporate phallus, there comes an urge to return to the good old days. And it is for that dream that lap dances were invented.

Unfortunately, the short answer is that lap-dancing clubs make idiots of all of us. If you are walking around with a hard-on and several hundred quid in your pocket, then there is always a club that will happily make your wallet lighter and your cock harder. But lap-dancing is the sexual equivalent of Chinese food – 20 minutes later, you're starving again. Famously, Robin Williams once said: "Cocaine is God's way of telling you that you're making too much money." Well, substitute the words "lap-dancing" for "cocaine", and "men" for "you", and you've got the picture.

There are few things more vulnerable than a man who finds himself loaded and horny in a foreign city far from home with nothing but an empty hotel room, a phone call to the missus and a porn film to look forward to. It is at this time that the Lords of Lap have you.

"Is there a club," you ask the cab driver in you best pidgin Spanish/French/Thai, "where you know a lonely business traveller

Menahem Kahana / AFP / Getty Images

might find a friendly face to share a cocktail, instead of resorting to the mini bar and a £5 packet of peanuts?"

So he takes you to the nearest titty bar, where, for the first half hour, you feel like Tony Montana, Don Corleone and Hugh Hefner rolled into one. The women are gorgeous, the drinks come oh-so-quickly with no sign of a bill, and when the hostess who you have been buying drinks for offers you a private dance… well, you'd have to be some sort of killjoy to refuse.

And then, four minutes later, you are £10 lighter and all you have is the brief memory of a pair of breasts waved several feet in front of your face and a vague feeling of arousal, yet further from any chance of satisfaction. And so you do it again. And again. Until you stumble from the club broke, drunk on overpriced booze, with the vague memory that your hotel's name begins with "El…" and a hard-on that no amount of porn can satisfy. However, if you're determined to spunk your cash where you'll, ahem, never get to spunk, here are a few rules to go by:

1. Never pay to get in. All lap-dancing clubs charge ludicrous entry fees. Simply refuse to pay. If you look like the kind of gent to drop a hundred quid on dances (and if you aren't, what the hell are you doing here?), then they will let you in for free.

2. Once in, chat and flirt, but do not have any lap dances. There is no need to pay to watch a honey, or a moose, gyrate 3ft away from you, when you can watch the same girl do it for free, 6ft away over someone else.

3. The best rule for lap-dancing clubs (apart from not going in the first place) is to get someone else to pay. There is no better money in the world when it comes to hedonism than other people's cash. And the best money with which to go to a lap-dancing club is that earned by a hedge-funder friend.

Otherwise, if you're really that horny, then you're better off going to a hooker. Or a real bar, where, who knows, you might even meet a real woman and fall in love. Then you're in for an even heftier bill – but at least you might get a shag. Lap dancers are like fruit machines that never pay out. Do not put your money in the slot.❖

The Craft of the Cad

By David Piper

David got fed up with treating women like shit, only
to be left with nothing but guilt in the morning, so
he set up the Cadogram Agency. He now leaves with
£500 in a brown envelope

QUITE WHETHER THE craft of caddery – one that seamlessly distils
dash (the cutting of a), thrust, elegance, panache, dynamism and out-
and-out, absolute, unapologetic, boundless rotterism into a single glint
of the eye – can be taught is highly questionable. Not least since good
looks cannot be learnt. One can but do one's bit for his brethren, though.

First, many men are bastards to women; others, sometimes called
gentlemen, are very kind and courteous. Women like both. The cad
combines – or confuses – the two in a sudden bewitching whirlwind,
and leaves a trail of marvellous, uplifting disappointment – heartbreak
with charm, untrustworthiness with sophistication, cruel rejection with
grace. Cads are irresistible paradoxes.

But it's not enough just to be incredibly charming and a bastard. You
must be the biggest bastard in the world, in the most stylish manner
possible, without being a bastard at all. You must stay blameless,
spotless in motive and pure of spirit. Your badness and goodness must
excite in equal measure.

You must be, even if you are not, many brilliant things – devilishly
handsome, a dashing hero or valiant, superior victim, experienced and
innocent, refined yet direct, fun, charismatic and capable of both great
elegance and impulsive, manly barbarity. You will be supremely
confident, but hide inside a (very useful) mess of problems (that you
absolutely need her help with). And remember, one of the best methods
of flirting with a lady (apart from generally being more brilliant than
one's surroundings) is to flirt brilliantly with other ladies. All cads are
incredible romantics and only ever want to find the right one (or two).

You must, in short, be a superlatively exciting prospect, through

Jan Schjetne/diggetydamn.com

varying proportions of perfection and danger. In the morning, or after neglecting to return her calls, or after you've kissed her best friend, the proportion of being perfect normally plummets. This calls for the cad's joker: his excuse. It's never our fault. Excuses can range from the blasé ("It's not my fault she was annoying and ugly" or "This is entirely the lady's fault, because I haven't changed"), to the ridiculous ("I will disappoint you only because you have disappointed me. You promised, even if only in my own imagination, to be more perfect than you are.

And that is immensely unfair on me"), to the far more cynical opportunity for tears and the revelation of vulnerability ("I'm sorry. I so desperately need to find love... yet look at what's become of me – I'm helpless, incapable of it... Even one night's company helps keep the pain away. Thank you.")

Let us consider feelings for a moment. Watch that you don't appear absolutely perfect, for this could inflict serious psychological damage on the lady. That would make you a really bad person, rather than the harmless spreader of joy that you are. Moreover, the closer a cad gets to intimating that he's an unabashed bounder (which has the inestimable benefit of making him more of a temptation to tame), the more the blame lies with the lady, who should know exactly what she's getting herself into.

> **'And remember: one of the best methods of flirting with a lady is to flirt brilliantly with other ladies'**

But it is precisely this moral mess that makes caddery such a conundrum to master. It takes quite a man to overcome his inevitable feelings of wretched, hollow guilt – not just because you've hurt someone innocent, but worse, because you know she thinks you're a shit (you know you're a shit, of course, but it's a lot easier to ignore if it seems the lady doesn't mind). And while most men like to think they would get away with slapping a girl's bottom in a club, there are far too many who find it impossible even to contemplate hurting a girl they don't yet hate. Moreover, very few men can ride the ridiculousness that comes with kissing a lady on the hand nowadays, and still come away looking attractive.

Still, if the mindset is mastered, the infinitely varied and subtle manifestations – "I say...!" – will come naturally. Practise kissing hands while on one knee and making little sleazy sneers or twinkles of the eye in the mirror. Ladies will see right through the act if you don't truly believe it is their manifest destiny to sleep with you tonight (and get kicked out, without a kiss, in the morning).

So come on, chaps, pull your socks up, get a haircut, learn how to shave, dress properly, dump those silly inhibitions and dare to be the blazing, eye-catching, verging-on-ridiculous, self-possessed winner of hearts and shatterer of illusions. For isn't it better to hurt many sparingly than to slowly foster immense hate for one or two over a lifetime? ❖

A Cock Is for Teasing

By Catherine Townsend

Catherine is the Independent's sex columnist and author of
Sleeping Around: Secrets of a Sexual Adventuress. She has shagged
on the first date, but concedes that sometimes it's better to wait

"DO YOU WANT a lap dance?" I was out with my male pals when
a gorgeous brunette with huge breasts started gyrating in front of me.
I nodded, completely entranced, as she peeled down to a microscopic
thong. The stripper was a cock tease, and that's why, hundreds of
pounds later, the boys were still drooling.

Cock tease. Some people say it like it's a bad thing. It entered the
vernacular in the 1800s as derogatory sexual slang for women who
tantalised men without delivering, but I'm starting to think that women
should reclaim the word. As a very hot economist told me, keeping men
wanting is like simple economics. "Men take anything – even sex – for
granted if they think the supply is unlimited," he said. "It's about
creating artificial scarcity."

I'm always up for a quickie in the shower, but lately, I've noticed my
lover has been treating my pussy like a Sky Plus box, assuming that he
can push "Play" whenever he likes. In today's everything-on-demand
culture, there's nothing wrong with savouring the build-up to sex. If
men don't get instant gratification, then they'll be begging you until
they get it – which puts all the power in your hands.

Being a cock tease, then, is about being all tits and no arse. You have
to offer a few smoke signals to indicate the promise of fire. Give out –
not that much, but enough to keep you number one. Seduce as you
refuse – you don't want to completely shut the door on them (we want
the goods too, after all). Try massaging your neck, for example, and
mention your exhausting yoga class, where you had your ankles behind
your head – that image will fuel his fantasies for weeks.

Every cock is there to tease. For the single girl, caving in reduces
your choices. Submit immediately, and he'll think, "That was easy.

I could probably do better." There's nothing sexy about being too sexually available. And once you put out, it's the only place a man goes. Hold him off with a charm offensive, however, and the dynamic changes completely – he'll think he's got the queen bee, and he'll treat you like one. A challenge is unquestionably irresistible to the ego – why else would ultra-powerful men be paying dominatrices in their lunch hour?

Long-term lovers can be hauled out of the man-shaped indentation in the sofa, too. It can be as simple as building anticipation with dirty e-mails. I'm a huge fan of the "accidental flash", where I pull up my dress, ostensibly adjusting something, so that my lover can get a glimpse of underwear. Then I send him off to work, knowing that the scene will be on constant replay in his head. Talking about sexual experiences can be a turn-on en route to the bedroom, but don't mention ex-lovers' prowess. When the male ego deflates, everything else soon follows suit.

> **❝Seduce as you refuse – you don't want to completely shut the door on them❞**

So when I realised I had become the Sky Plus box, I decided to make my lover work for it. I started by calling him to let him know how wet I was, and that I was touching myself. Just as he was heating up, I made my excuses and went to dinner with my girlfriends. I had four missed calls and several naughty texts. Then, back at his place, I stripped down to a thong and heels and gave him a lap dance, tying his hands behind his back so he couldn't touch me. Eventually, I moved him to the bed, where I tied him to the bedposts (some people like handcuffs, but I find them too easy to escape from, unless you use police handcuffs, and they're a nightmare if you lose the key; I prefer silk scarves). I pushed my breasts in his face, sat on top of him and made him lick me until I had an orgasm. Finally, when I had him begging for it, I gave him a blow job. But just as he was building up to a climax, I took a break and went to the bathroom to paint my nails. Then I masturbated myself while he watched. The more I made him wait, the more turned on I felt. The tie-up tease is an amazing way to guarantee you multiple orgasms.

But it's not just all about me. The art of the cock tease – and the deferral of gratification – makes for more sensitivity on both sides, richer fantasies, more sexual charge and better sex all round. This is tantric sex with tassels.❖

Jackpot (©2006) courtesy of Foley Gallery, NY / Thomas Barry Fine Arts, MN
Thomas Allen

The Straight Man's Guide to Cruising

By Paul Flynn

Paul is a journalist and an A-gay

FOR THE DEFINITIVE manual on the benefits of cruising, read The Orton Diaries. They're a blast! Joe Orton, the playwright, humorist and deeply irreverent intellectual, was a cruiser of distinction. From 1966 to 1967, he intimately documented his wordless encounters. Yet all of them – from fucking Irish navvies down alleys to a spot of mild fellatio on the way back from buying the Sunday papers – come with a caveat loud and clear. Orton was bludgeoned to death by his boyfriend in his apartment. While his diaries might tell a different tale, his final departure suggests that the gay habit for having one's cake and sucking it isn't always a given.

It's not for lack of trying. Having grown up isolated by feelings of difference, exclusion and secrecy, the gay community developed its own semi-Masonic sign language for picking one another up in unusual locations. In the same way that a dog whistle is only audible to canines, the codified signals of cruising are largely undetectable to the untrained eye. Most people have no idea how many men are giving each other the come-on in locker rooms and on public transport.

But judging from the number of tan marks spotted on ring fingers in cruising hotspots, there's evidently also something of a straight following. Be it in a sauna, a public lavatory, on the street, in a park or by the handy device of a webcam, cruising starts with direct eye contact. And it's a look that sits at the exact meeting point between menace and arousal. Then there's a rustle of the trouser, a hand in the back pocket, a casual nod of the head, a light tap on the shoulder, a deeply phoney "All right mate" that could be taken either way.

Cruising is a swift business. Once eye contact has been maintained and the initial beckon reciprocated, the less conversation the better. One encounter in its entirety may consist of the six words, "You got a place to go?" usually delivered two octaves below regulation speech pitch. Then, once a location has been established, it is very much down to business.

Orton wasn't the only famous gay with a penchant for this psychosexual role play. George Michael espouses it with unabashed regularity. When caught by a paparazzo in a compromising situation with a man who looked like he ought to be called Brian (but strangely wasn't), Michael made a delightfully bold pronouncement. "This is our culture," he proclaimed, thus holding the whole of the gay world to account in his defence.

But is it? The received thinking is that cruising now lives in a neutered bubble. And it is in bathhouses – once the famed seat of cruising for 1970s San Franciscans – where most cruising, ahem, goes down around the world. These super-saunas are deemed perfectly acceptable punctuation points of a gay night out. The casual sex booths, the porn cinemas, the steam rooms, the tiny towels barely covering a host of genitalia, from the most to the least impressive, and the whirlpool baths with hands always underwater are the new zenith of cruising culture. Online, the pre-eminence of Gaydar.co.uk and its international counterparts, Manhunt.net and the rather less poetically titled Men4SexNow.com, have made the traditional booty call something akin to ordering a slice of Domino's pizza. The mystique is disappearing.

Some of the bemoaning stems from the fact that gay men now have to pay for the pleasure of having their cruising policed and private. Gone is the happy sight of bobbing homosexual heads and backsides dotted across the urban landscape, following a crackdown of outdoor cruising (and a cut-down of friendly trees and bushes). But what straight man has not yearned for the idea of sex on tap? Who can honestly say that if there were a spot, be it a sauna or a website, where willing women were ready for no-strings encounters, they wouldn't indulge?

The rise of straight cruising – or "dogging", as it is called, with such a massive air of animalistic desperation – looks ghastly. The truth is that straight cruising has yet to find its class. It has yet to have its own Orton. How to cruise as a straight man? Wedding rings off, boys.❖

Rough Sex – a Guide

By Rebecca Newman

Rebecca is GQ's sex shrink. Strictly in the name of research, she has explored the kink scenes of the world

IMAGINE YOURSELF PINNED up against a wall being ravished by someone you love. Picture yourself being forced to come again and again, though you're begging for mercy and can hardly see through the stars. Romance and rose petals are all very well. But just as great seduction involves being overwhelmed, so does great sex.

At entry level, it need be nothing more than a Rhett Butler embrace, clasping his "Scarlett" in his strong arms, or the girl from accounts pulling the boss by his tie into the stationery cupboard. The core of the game is not pain. It's power – the wild rush of wresting control to inflict erotic delight and the angry, helpless, horny sensation of being consensually "forced" to obey.

Dallying in the shallows of high heels and the occasional silk scarf may be as far as you want to go. If you think that you would hate to be bitten, maybe this just isn't for you. But is it possible that you have never had someone find your threshold, and expertly toy with you right at the edge?

Crossing the line to real rough stuff isn't easy. To dominate someone takes all of your being: as they give themselves to you, so you give everything back. Negotiation is crucial, as are "safe" words that defend your nuclear no-go areas. The submissive partner can wail, "Stop", content he'll be ignored, but confident that if he shouts, "Red light", you'll drop everything (unless, of course, you've hung him from the ceiling in the intricate knots of Japanese *shibari* rope bondage).

Now the science bit. The goal is to trigger the release of endorphins – opiates produced naturally by excitement or duress. Elegantly executed, this can make you as high as the finest E. Beware, however: the comedown the next day is equally potent. In dungeon-speak it is known as "subdrop", a childlike state in which you are reduced to a clingy, muddled heap. Allow for an afternoon under the duvet with dark

Paul Davis

chocolate and old movies.

So let us imagine you're a woman who knows what she wants (and these techniques work equally well guy-on-girl or girl-on-girl, with the odd minor adaptation). Peel off your stockings and use them to tie a willing man to your bed. The endorphins must kick in before he can handle heavy sensation, so begin slowly, teasing him with the merest breath over his skin, the lightest touch of your lips.

As he becomes aroused, he'll be able to handle more. Reach for your props. Don't skimp on these: nothing beats the smell and texture of expensive leather. Turn his face to one side, pressing his cheek into the pillow, limiting what he is able to see. Bite along the flesh of his shoulders. Twist his nipples, then take them gently between your teeth as you drag your nails over the sensitive sides of his waist. Once his entire upper body is taut with excitement, run your hands down to grip the top of his thighs – always maintain contact – and softly take the length of his cock into your mouth. Untie his legs so you can reach the curve where his buttocks meet the back of his legs. This "sweet spot" is especially receptive to spanking. Run your hands over the area to warm it up, then spank upwards, with only a small degree of force at first. When you land the stroke, keep your palm on him with firm pressure as he flinches, then pause – anticipation is all – and repeat, largo con passione, in a rhythmic tempo.

If he likes this, consider knife play, with the cold of the blade flat against his skin; temperature play, in which wax and ice used together will confuse his nervous system and bend his mind; or full-blown flagellation: many-tailed deerskin floggers land with a delicious, thudding impact, whereas canes and whips give a sharp, stinging blow. Then, for rainy days, there's electricity play and blood-letting. The more intensely you work, the more you must wrap yourself around your submissive. Breathe as he breathes, feel what he feels. For the duration, nothing else exists.

Surrender yourself to someone you trust and abandon your inhibitions. This is a sophisticated pursuit that challenges the boundaries, an expression of love every bit as much as decorous love-making. In Dangerous Liaisons, the Marquis de Merteuil speaks sooth: "Don't you know that however willing we are to give ourselves, we must nevertheless have an excuse? And is there any more convenient than the appearance of yielding to force?" ❖

Sex Party Etiquette

By Catherine Townsend

Catherine is a sex columnist and sexplorer

"DO YOU WANT to play with us?" Perched on a round bed with dozens of horny strangers writhing in ecstasy around me, I couldn't help but feel terrified. I was the Sex Party Novice. I wanted to kiss the stunning, lithe brunette who was stroking my thighs, but since she was already mid-coitus, I faltered. Somehow, "You have great tits but your date has way too much back hair" seemed a bit inappropriate.

I'm glad I hesitated. Far from being a free-for-all, there is often a strict code of conduct – and if you flout, you're out. Sometimes it's only women who can make the advances. At many parties, guy-on-guy action is usually discouraged, while girls can take their pick, girls or guys. Sometimes men aren't allowed to approach at all, and single men are often frankly NFI. Asking the hostess for the rules and reading the website guidelines is vital. Positive discrimination continues with ticket prices – it's usually cheapest for single girls. And single women are always the most in demand. At times, I have felt like a piece of flesh being dangled in front of hungry alligators.

> **❛Exploits can go on until dawn and while I've never played with more than two strangers (honest), I've seen up to 15 people entwined in a sticky situation❜**

You're right to imagine Eyes Wide Shut. Most sex parties I've attended have been held in private homes and the addresses are e-mailed on the day; I've also been asked to e-mail photos for "evaluation" by a committee. Exploits can go on until dawn, and while I've never played with more than two strangers (honest), I've seen up to

Dan Burn-Forti/danburnforti.com

15 people entwined in a sticky situation. Nervous? Find a regular to help you navigate virgin territory – they'll most likely get off on it.

Proceedings usually open with a clothes-on cocktail party – now is not the best time to discuss politics, dispute global warming or ask if someone's breasts are real. A delicate balance of inebriation should be struck: enough to loosen inhibitions without deadening everything below the waist. Some women wear elaborate costumes, but I usually opt for my little black dress – flattering, comfortable and, crucially, easy to remove. I once made the rookie error of putting on my knickers before my fishnets, which meant that I couldn't take them off and ended up tripping over my shoes. Men have it much easier. They just have to ensure pants aren't stained and socks aren't left on.

Inevitably, people start disappearing to various playrooms: rooms with lots of beds, couches or just one super-sized bed. (NB: it's not really about coupling off – that defeats the purpose.) Rules are rigid: no cameras, no phones, no prostitutes, no loud conversation. If someone invites you "to take a look around" or "to come through with us", it's an invitation to play. If everyone is starkers, just strip off, climb onto one of the beds and allow your hands to wander to what they like (thighs, arms and backs are preferable to the it-bits as an overture).

Most guests don't take it personally if you politely remove a wayward hand, nor should you they: after all, not everyone's fantasy is the same. And nonverbal communication is safest. Clicking with someone in conversation can make rejecting them more awkward. "Maybe later" will soften the blow. If a person or couple politely declines, don't persist. You have one more strike. There is always voyeurism (remember, you're surrounded by exhibitionists). For a good show, there's usually some watersport action in the bathrooms, but note that "domestics" make for very bad shows; they're a serious libido killer. If with your partner, ensure you're both on the same page before heading out. And if you don't desire any interaction whatsoever, best stay home and keep your porn collection company.

Condoms are crucial (unless on complicit, closed sets) and it's advisable to bring your own. The organisers usually provide them, but you don't want to have to miss out on hot action should stocks expire – and it's always "one woman, one condom". Breaking the condom rule is usually route one to a red card.

Recognising someone you know with their trousers down can be amusing. Follow the Fight Club rule and don't broach the subject on "the outside". Protecting secrets allows people to lose their inhibitions – and we like that. Of course, there are always disguises, though these can backfire. A girlfriend once peed on a guy in a mask only to discover he was her uncle. But whether it was a surprise visit from Bob in accounting or mysterious strangers, don't forget to thank everyone for a jolly good servicing. ❖

How to Handle a Hooker

By Sebastian Horsley

Sebastian is an artist, the author of Dandy in the Underworld and "the man who slept with a 1,000 prostitutes". Actually, it's more like 1,200

I REMEMBER THE first time I had sex – I still have the receipt. The girl was alive, as far as I could tell: she had a warm body, and she was better than nothing. She cost me £20. I remember thinking that I could have strangled her for £50. I was 16 then and I'm 44 now. I have spent 25 years throwing my money and heart at tarts. I have slept with every nationality in every position in every country. I am a connoisseur of prostitution: I can take its bouquet, taste it, roll it around my mouth, give you the vintage. I have used brothels, saunas, private homes found on the internet and ordered girls to my flat prompt as pizza. While we are on the subject, I have also run a brothel. And I have been a male escort.

I wish I were more ashamed.

But I'm not. You see, I love prostitutes and everything about them. They are the most honest and open people on God's earth. For a dandy, whores soon cease to be what they are for most bores – a substitute for regular women. It is regular women that are a substitute – and a poor one – for prostitutes. Here, you get the sensation of sex without the boredom of its conveyance. Ergo, you will have fun. Brothels are magical places. They enable astounding physical intimacy without the intervention of personality. I love the artificial paradise of them: the anonymity, the squalor and the use of money (that most impersonal instrument of intimacy) to buy the ultimate act of intimacy. It's lust over love, sensation over security and the opportunity to fall into a woman's arms without falling into her hands.

So here's how to go about it.

The Walk-Ups In Amsterdam, the girls all stand in the windows shimmering, as tantalising as tropical fish beyond the gleam of aquarium glass. But in London, you can't see them, so there's always the exhilaration of not knowing what you're going to get. A fuck in Soho will cost you £25, the same fuck £50 in Shepherd Market, Mayfair. Strangely, there is no real correlation between price and quality in the business of selling pleasure. I have fucked whores as gorgeous as Raquel Welch for £25 and as hideous as Ann Widdecombe for £200. The abnormalities in the market would have confused even Mr Keynes. Shop around. Always tip the maid at least £2. And always, always be polite. I believe in manners – even though I am a cannibal, I do say Grace.

The Saunas There are hundreds of places scattered over the country where you can get raped and have a sauna at the same time. The first thing you need to do is buy McCoy's British Massage Parlour Guide. This is the Egon Ronay volume for the professional fornicator. I made it a point of principle to visit every single establishment in London, and so should you. In the more expensive ones, the girls parade in front of you one by one, like bowls of sushi on a carousel. It is very sweet. And fucking in a sauna is very exciting. It's also a levelling experience. It's not the heat, it's the humility.

The Escort Agencies Go to the internet or Yellow Pages. Call-outs are more expensive (about £250 for a house visit; most take credit cards), but the big difference between sex for money and sex for free is that sex for money usually costs a lot less. What's nice about this experience is that you can order your dream girl – squaw, doormat, trophy, Barbie – just like that. Also, you've got more chance of a kiss. Hookers, like wives, don't kiss. A kiss is like a job application made on the top floor for a position going in the basement. With whores, the basement is permanently let, but the top floor is locked.

So have fun, my darlings. And remember, don't listen to those awful liberal-minded, fatty feminist-flag-waving doom-mongers who say prostitution is evil. Who are we to tell someone what parts of themselves they can and cannot sell? If we make a choice to sell our minds and souls to the highest bidder, but give our bodies away for free, why should we think it wrong if someone did the opposite? Sex is one of the most wholesome, spiritual and natural things that money can buy. ❖

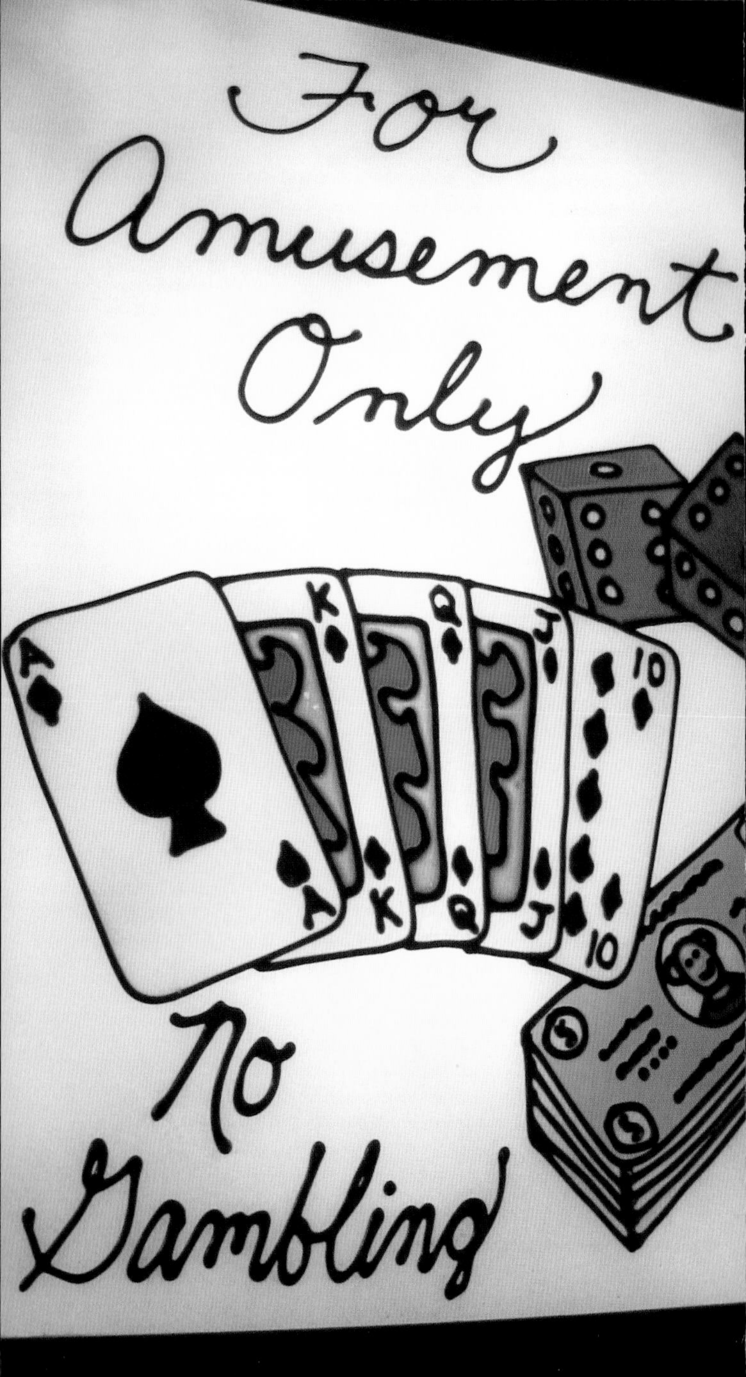
For
Amusement
Only
No
Gambling

5

Play

' Blessed are the flexible,
for they shall not
be bent out of shape '

Anonymous

Opposite: PJ Chmiel

Less Is Never More
By Camilla Morton

Camilla, fashion writer and authoress of A Girl for All Seasons,
sees Manolos as necessity, Dior as her comfort blanket and
couture as the perfect antidote for stage fright

LOOK AWAY NOW, shrinking violets. Pass the smelling salts, because
less is never more. When it comes to glamour, to spending, to shopping,
to style, to you, to me, why be stingy? What joy is there in "less" when
there is always "more" to be had? We want it all, so why not just have it
all? Think Edith Piaf, "Je ne regrette rien"– live La Vie en Rose lifestyle.

Love luxury, because luxury is "more", likewise, love couture, love
one-offs – these *objets recherchés* have the power to elevate you from the
crowd. This soaring effect proves that retail therapy is a more genuinely
gratifying high than any other kick. And instead of waking up feeling all
"morning after", you have a brand new friend (or, better still, an entire
wardrobe of friends) that you actually want to get to know, rather than
just wishing they'd disappear from the adjacent pillow.

Don't worry, this is not some fluffy fashion rot out to persuade you
that a pair of shoes can change the world, or that a couture dress can
and will deliver all you desire – though it has, of course (did you learn
nothing from Cinderella?). But there is much to be said for the cheering
effect of luxury on the soul. And there is no such thing as saving it for
best – make every day a better day by spoiling yourself.

Budget, did I hear you splutter? What is a budget? Is it beyond your
dreams? You have to spend money to make money. As Oscar Wilde
once said: "Anybody who lives within their means suffers from a lack of
imagination." Credit cards were invented for a reason – it is your duty
to the economy to spend and keep everyone in jobs. Think of all the
Christmas bonuses and hungry mouths that depend on your decadence.

Why not offset your indulgences and excess with good deeds and kindness, such as donating last season's wardrobe to charity. And while you're still feeling extravagant, be sure to spend even more on gifts. Less is never more, particularly with giving. From kisses to Tiffany boxes, always go for big gestures. Better to give, give, give and then see what you might receive…

But let's get to the nitty-gritty – how to live it. Remember, phones were invented to be used, taxis designed to be taken and five-star hotels are there just waiting for you to check into them. Take a sickie to have a spree: you are, after all, ministering your own mental health. To charge it is to cure it. Saving for a rainy day is frankly, in these climes, very unnecessary. Then there is always Someone Else's Credit Card. Note that partners are like knickers – there's the dime-a-dozen or the top end. You are aiming for silks, satins, La Perlas and purrrfection.

So if life is getting a little too serious – that's what reality does to you – live it up. If you feel intimidated, dress it up. When creating a visual impact, less is – you've guessed it – never more. Scare with style, not long words so obscure that conversations have to be paused while your musings are Googled. An abundant décolletage is much more effective at getting across an instant message. No need to reply. This theory applies to colour, too, which is a very direct way of out-fashioning any potential "situation". Red lips = look, don't touch. Red shoes = you're coming home with me tonight. Red dress = you don't stand a chance. All three? You'll have anybody you want at "hello". Less is only more when we're talking material coverage on a woman's body; for example, a micro-mini by Azzedine Alaïa.

> **'Think of all the Christmas bonuses and hungry mouths that depend on your decadence'**

True, it's trickier for men. Not only are women far more complex – remember less is never ever more when it comes to compliments, flowers and phone calls – alas, the male wardrobe is usually a bit lacking and has fewer options (why is it that only gay men feel comfortable being stylish?). But don't neglect it, particularly if you hope of ever having someone to look after you. Try rather than worry, or if you really have no style, just throw your money at gadgets, gizmos and housekeepers, and on lavishing your arm candy. Girls can take care of "less is never more" for you, if it helps. Just remember, as the saying goes, you're worth it. ❖

Designer: Aina Hussein, model: Urszula (Oxygen Models, London)
Jan Schjetne / diggetydamn.com

Get Ahead in the Art World

By Nick Hackworth

Nick is an art critic, gallerist and an expert in 1970s
East German soft-porn movie soundtracks

"HELLO YOU CUNT" was, reportedly, the young Damien Hirst's
opening gambit deployed at a private view against the late fashionista
and art fan Isabella Blow. In response, she turned to her companion and
said, "See, I told you he was a genius," suggesting that our first rule for
success in the art world is **always to be charming**.

Requiring a little more commitment from the art-world hopeful is
adherence to the advice that **it's always a good idea to be German**.
Throughout the ages, this has been a highly effective strategy employed
by creatives such as Goethe and Wagner, who wanted to tap into that
longstanding Germanic quality of *Sturm und Drang*, ie being extremely
serious and romantic (not in the Barbara Cartland sense). This is
working very well for Anselm Kiefer, the current heavyweight champion
of Germanic seriousness and creator of some of the world's heaviest
(in metric tons) artworks, which always seem to threaten disaster,
mainly due to the structural integrity of the buildings that house them.
If you do choose to emulate Kiefer, you might like to **buy a Latin
and/or Ancient Greek dictionary**, as Kiefer and the old American
abstract master Cy Twombly have clearly done. You can then score a
double whammy of seriousness by scrawling classical phrases across
your paintings, thus showing that, culturally speaking, you are equally at
home resting in the shade of the Athenian stoa listening to Socrates as
you are wandering Teutonic forests at twilight. Confusingly, for those
attached to the primitive cultural stereotype that Germans have no
sense of humour, a winning variant of this overall strategy is to **be a
funny German**, like the late Martin Kippenberger, whose paintings are
widely regarded as hilarious for no apparent reason. Nonetheless,
deadpan cynicism and an ironic relationship to cultural seriousness are

Jill Calder / jillcalder.com

working well for many Germans, including a group known as the Leipzig painters and individual nutters like Jonathan Meese.

Astonishingly, a number of the aforementioned Leipzig painters seem to have got away with ignoring our next rule, which is that **it's best to be technically incompetent** (especially if you're going to be a painter or a video artist). According to the highly reasonable and not-at-all-historically-illiterate thinking of the art-world intelligentsia, actual skills are the preserve of evil aristocrats and nasty Western fascist-colonialist-imperialists who want to enslave the world to capitalist markets and force people to draw bowls of fruit forever. Therefore, to **show resistance to the powers that be** (in itself a very good idea), try to be completely talentless. Only the highest adepts of this path are able to reach that holy place found at the confluence of technical incompetence, intellectual vacuity and spiritual shallowness. Find it, and you've found the art world's El Dorado (NB: if you're a video artist, try leaving on the lens cap).

In an increasingly competitive global market, the result of a staggering rise over the past decade in the numbers of participants in the art world, **differentiation is vital as a source of competitive advantage**. This can be achieved by cultivating an interest in an obscure subculture as a source for your work. This fact has resulted in the cultural equivalent of a vicious arms race, in which artists, critics and curators have sought to discover, colonise and exploit increasingly obscure subcultures, giving rise to terrifying levels of specialisation. It is no longer sufficient to foster an interest in, say, 1970s East German soft-porn movies, but necessary to travel further and develop an expertise in, to stay with our example, the *soundtracks* of 1970s East German soft-porn movies. Thus armed, you may make your terrible work/write your text/curate your thematically based show in supreme confidence.

In a similar vein, it's also essential to **acquire an intimidating library of theoretical texts**. This will viscerally illustrate your interest in critical theory without actually necessitating any actual knowledge. The best book by far to own, talk about and ostentatiously look at meaningfully is A Thousand Plateaus by French theoretical combo Deleuze and Guattari, as nobody has ever read it. If, in philosophical discussion, force of argument fails you, or your challenger notices that your library is mainly made up of fake polystyrene books, simply use force and literally beat your ideological enemy over the head with an appropriate text. For this I would recommend GEM De Ste Croix's seminal study The Class Struggle in the Ancient Greek World, as it a) proves your cultural and intellectual breadth, b) conveniently highlights your dedication to the socialist struggle and c) is very heavy.❖

Join the Jet Set

By Oscar Humphries

Oscar is a failed social climber whose address
book shrinks like the waning moon

LIFE IN THE jet set is an endless stream of boats, planes, beautiful
women, conspicuously dressed men and exotic animal skins made into
horrible clothes. Their life is dedicated to pleasure: one long group
holiday that dot-to-dots its way across the Med in the summer
(anywhere with a mooring for the gin palace – Monaco, Cannes, "St
Tro", Ibiza); in the winter, Gstaad, St Moritz and St Barts; and in
between, breathers at the Meadows, the Priory or some Scientology
"chill-out facility". But they're not simply chasing the sun and each
other. They're after non-stop fun – with money to burn, models to shag
and cars to drive too fast, frantically trying to mask their insecurity by
surrounding themselves with life's more obvious luxuries. They are not
the Valentinos and Elle Macphersons of this world – they are the
people who aspire to be like them, or with them. It's not a hard club to
infiltrate: all you need to be is very attractive and willing to sleep with
morbidly unattractive men. Or be rich, or appear rich.

Buy a Rolex Jet-setters love a watch – ironic, considering their
disregard for punctuality and distinct lack of pressing appointments.
The bigger the better: the hard-to-find Rolex Daytona in steel, the
Hublot Big Bang, Audemars Piguets and Panerais. Fakes can easily be
sourced online, but beware: while the jet set don't know much about
anything, they know where to buy Tod's loafers in Cannes and they
know watches.

Quit your job The jet set don't work. They acquire. They invest.
They are invested in. The girls start niche fashion labels. The boys are
in the shady world of oil or minerals. Or they "just chill". The only 9-5
they know is their tanning regime. They might work a little over long
lunches at Club 55 in St Tropez via their BlackBerry until the nightclub

promoters summon them. Play with your PDA a bit and it will be assumed you're managing your mineral-extraction empire.

Go shopping Shopping, along with topping up tans, getting laid and keeping up with each other, is their *raison d'être*. The men wear frayed jeans, a shirt open to the navel and loafers without socks. Their fashion icons are Gatsby, Studio 54's Steve Rubell and Flavio Briatore, possibly the worst-dressed human being on this and any planet – now, then and forever... and ever. The girls are a little better. They love an It bag and a bit of Louboutin and Jimmy Choo (but can't quite muster the courage to ask Eurotrash's poster girl Tamara Mellon – who they met once – for a discount).

Invest in property The jet set live everywhere and nowhere. Ask where they're from and they'll ask back, "How long have you got?" only to reel off names of places and schools and rehab clinics in a mid-Atlantic accent. Buy a place in New York, St Tropez and London, an Argentinean cattle station and a house in the Hamptons. Buy a private plane, a big yacht and a Riva Aquarama to get you to the boat.

Find a mate The guys like models or, if their oil business has gone belly up, will settle for an ugly heiress with models on the side. The girls

Carlo Allegri/Getty Images

like art dealers, polo players and boys they went to school with.

Go to a party The jet set have panic attacks if they think they've failed to make a guest list or, worse, gone to an inferior party. There are even agencies to get you into Eurotrash hot spots. But blaggers, beware: if caught out, the jet set could try and interrogate you (over dinner at Harry's Bar). Memorise the following:

Boys Your favourite film is… Scarface. You love the scene at the end with all the coke and the guns. Your favourite book is… anything by Bret Easton Ellis, apart from the last one, which you found a bit weird and "quite hard". Your favourite sexual position is…doggy. Yeah baby, yeah! Your favourite designer is… Flavio Briatore. He has the best taste of anybody ever, anywhere, ever… Your fantasy dinner guest…Gisele. They will "high five" you at this point and you'll be in.

Girls Your favourite book is… you have never read a book in your life. And will never do so. Your favourite sexual position is… whatever the nice man in the sealskin bomber wants. Your favourite designer is…Cavalli or Jitrois. Your favourite restaurant is… you last ate solids in 2001. Your favourite song is… anything by Jay-Z, who you met through James Blunt, who you met through Petra Nemcova.❖

How to Be a Star

By Andrew Stone

Andrew is the editor-in-chief of Los Angeles Confidential
magazine, author of A Hedonist's Guide to New York and
a very reluctant celebrity connoisseur

WHILE IT'S EASY to rag on celebrities for their unsavoury antics,
let's get real. You've fantasised about air-kissing Iman and David as they
stroll into a gallery opening. Wouldn't it be nice to be waved through
the velvet ropes as a jealous line of average Joes looks on? So satisfying
to open your favourite glossy and see yourself smiling back? If I were
to dig really deep, I could hypothesize about fear of death (Irene Cara
put it so eloquently: "Fame, I wanna live forever…"), but in the spirit of
generosity, I'll just point out some winning ways to fame. Maybe, with a
bit of hard work, you too can have Jay-Z's number in your Sidekick.

Step 1: **Idolatry**

Pick the star whose public persona impresses you the most and act like
them. I have a philosophy called WWKMD (What Would Kate Moss
Do?). When in a socially intimidating situation, I affect aloofness by
whispering to my companions, making frequent trips to the powder
room and focusing into the distance as if in deep thought. Whether in
a nightclub or the hardware store, I try to imagine the world as one big
CK One advert.

Step 2: **Maintenance**

If you really want to roll among the stars and pseudo-celebs, you must
invest in dental bleaching, microdermabrasion, beach-body boot camp
and/or core-fusion intensives, a spiritual adviser, a coif created by Sally
Hershberger kicked up with Tom Ford hair perfume and – above all else
– the right high-end accessories. Real celebrities – not to mention all the
shop assistants at Chanel, Prada and John Varvatos – can tell if you're a

James Muldowney

fake by your shoes, watch, belt, bag and sunglasses. It's the details that make you godly.

Step 3: Brand Image

You are a product, and you must become an expert in product placement. When at a hot spot – particularly one patrolled by paparazzi – don't converse with unattractive people, unless they own a fashion house, art gallery, modelling agency or record label. If you manage to get photographed for the "Out and About" pages, try to smile with insouciance. Think to yourself, "Of course I belong here." Follow this up by spelling your name slowly and clearly to the photographer and making him spell it back to you. There is no worse slight than being labelled "Guest" in the caption.

Step 4: The Rules of Engagement

Never appear impressed by anybody, whether it's the cutest girl in the bar or Sofia Coppola at the Chateau Marmont. If you orbit them like they're Jupiter and you're one of its moons, they will make sure you never land in their line of vision again. So even if Orlando Bloom bums a cigarette off you or Natalia Vodianova thinks your shoes are cool, just act as if they're anybody else. If you feel bold, tell Orlando you like his watch. This allows the conversation to stretch a tad longer, though do not take this as an open invitation to join him on his banquette.

Have a few talking points at the ready, however. You're considering going on a Zen retreat with Deepak Chopra that Vikram Chatwal is throwing together. You've got a few film projects on – one is loosely based on your crazy life, another is a documentary about migrant workers in Kashmir. You're working with Bono on the 2010 Live Earth concert in Shanghai, though details are totally unofficial at the moment. Do not tell the truth, that you work at Beach Bum Tanning and live alone with three cats. If they crack a joke, laugh – but do not overdo it. Like a deer in your backyard, the slightest move may cause them to scamper away.

Step 5: **Desperate Measures**

Men, it may come down to your wallet. See that table of models over there? Send over a bottle of Grey Goose or Patron. They will, in all likelihood, gladly accept it. Once they've consumed at least half, saunter over and "see if they're enjoying it". It may be your lucky day. If they give you the finger, shrug it off with grace. Demanding pussy may well have you removed by the bouncer. This will not help your cause.

Ladies, you have a few options. You can create a "wardrobe malfunction", à la Janet Jackson or Tara Reid, and allow a breast to pop out. You can collide with the hottest man in the room and hope he finds it charming. Or, if all else fails, throw a drink in the face of the highest profile man there and scream, "Don't touch me!" ❖

The Ten Commandments of Surf God-dom

By Jamie Brisick

Jamie is a lapsed surf god and the author of Have Board, Will Travel: The Definitive History of Surf, Skate and Snow

I Thou Shalt Never Miss a Swell

Unlike most sports where the playing field is static, surfing is built upon a set of fickle variables that include swell, wind and tide. The Surf God (or SG) is therefore a slave to nature's whims – his entire life is designed around making a beeline for the surf at the expense of everything else. Which means a steady job is out of the question (doesn't matter, this is "the best job in the world" – though few have had any other). Which means he has far too much time on his hands. Which means a lolloping, slooow demeanour and drawling, teenage speech, thus…

II Thou Shalt Talk the Talk

Ever noticed how surfers tend to overuse the words "like", "super" and "siiick"? It's partly due to spending too much time in the sun; partly because one can be only so acrobatic in life, and better to do it in the surf than on the tongue; and partly because, thanks to the first commandment, the myopic pursuit of surf negates the need for any other interests beyond what the waves are doing, bro. Hence, the SG has little to say for himself.

III Thou Shalt Downplay One's Heroic Feats

There is tremendous ego and braggadocio among SGs, but it is veiled in passive-aggressiveness. For instance, 12-15ft surf will be called "eight-to-ten", a nine-second tube ride is a "semi cover-up", a 6ft air is merely a "bunny hop" and a near-death pummelling by a Waimea Bay clean-up set is shrugged off as "no big deal, s'only water".

IV Thou Shalt Expose Chest and Reveal a Hint of Ass Crack

You're familiar with those low-slung, knee-length board shorts? Well, a little secret – it's a serious case of form over function. They get hooked on the knees and they strait-jacket the thighs. But because surfing is as much about image as athleticism, thou shalt never be seen in Speedos or Lycra cycling shorts.

V Thou Shalt Enjoy Bongs Between Sessions

When the yoga-practising, psychedelic soldiers of the 1970s broke new ground at Pipeline, they were often high on weed or acid. A decade later, when they brought small-wave moves to the heaving tubes of remote Indonesia, their relaxation under pressure was aided by smoking opiates. And though the sport has become somewhat puritanical in recent years, the true SG still puffs.

VI Thou Shalt Not Eat Shark

Tuna, halibut, sea bass, swordfish and even mahi-mahi can be consumed with finger-licking gluttony. But for God's sake, keep the man in the grey suit as far from one's dinner plate as possible. It's not only ancient Hawaiian superstition, it's biblical: do unto others…

VII Thou Shalt Be a Messenger

In the same way as you can hold a conch shell to the ear and hear the ocean, so too can you look into a SG's eyes and be instantly transported to the sand, sun and surf. Some call it the "walk-on-water effect", others simply "afterglow". Landlocked housewives call it an aphrodisiac.

VIII Thou Shalt Be a Bit of a Failure in the Relationship Department

This can be done a couple of ways. The SG can either remind his girlfriend verbally that surfing is No 1 (which will either kill the relationship or create distance), or he can simply become a big-wave hell-charger, which will force her to reconcile the fact that he could die at any minute and that she may as well quit now to save herself the pain.

IX Thou Shalt Be a Surf Fundamentalist

The SG must regard his chosen faith as the be-all and end-all and

Tony Alva Muir Vidler

preach the good word. This is both ambassadorial and self-preservationist. Because of the tremendous sacrifice involved in rising to SG status (college, career and general interest in the world all out the window), the "endless summer" must be endlessly defended both to others and oneself.

X Thou Shalt Travel

Inherent to the surfing life is the Search for the Perfect Wave. Which means today's SG will come to know Australia, South Africa, Tahiti, Fiji, France, Brazil, Chile, Hawaii and many more exotic, wave-rich coastlines on his journey to God-dom. And this is the pay-off: when his rippled chest and dazzling cutbacks have been declared bankrupt (note the SG's early sell-by date, as he is tossed back to civilian life in his early thirties when the next generation of whippersnappers render him obsolete), it will be these memories, this waterborne worldliness that will become his greatest asset. ❖

What You Can Really Get out of Concierge

By Imogen Edwards-Jones

Imogen is the author of Hotel Babylon, 'a journey through the entrails of the luxury hotel business'

THERE'S NO SUCH thing as "no" in the hotel industry. All the top hotels boast that they can provide anything as long as it's legal. And at some, also à la carte are nose candy, hookers – hell, even a sacrificial sheep for your suite barbecue as one Saudi once demanded (and got) in a five-star London hotel. It's just a question of asking nicely – and giving good tip.

You'll find the concierge behind a desk in reception, usually wearing a (hard-earned) Golden Key motif on both lapels. He is, after the manager (and you, of course), the Most Important Person in the hotel. He is also the gatekeeper to your pleasures. If you want to jump the three-month waiting list for a table at The Ivy, have your dress dry-cleaned at midnight, get 30 Dolce Vita long-stemmed roses in an hour or fill a bath with 48 bottles of Evian and a couple of prostitutes, he's your man. And he will neither complain nor bat an eyelid. All you need do is cross his palm with notes and he'll be your very best friend.

But you need the right hotel first. The male models that work in design hotels couldn't get you a booking at McDonald's; that boutique hotel with just six super-luxe rooms for missionary-position couples won't have the connections or the buying power to source, say, seven hookers from each continent. No, the bastions are the best – just follow the high-spending Texans, Arabs and expense-account businessmen. And the uglier and older the concierge, the better he'll be: the gnarled one with the gold tooth will get you everything. Apart from, that is, impartial advice — he's on backhanders from everywhere: cabs, theatres, restaurants (the concierge's reward – the tip plus the backhander – is known as the "double bubble").

A good concierge can make more than £3,000 a month in tips and kickbacks, so gratuities must be competitive. No standard-issue 12%, thank you very much – make it more like 20% and you'll get the wink. But don't expect to stroll up to the desk waving a note to get your gram and girl. You need to establish a relationship and "earn" their trust. On arrival, slip them a crisp fifty and introduce yourself: "I'm here for the weekend, I'm planning to spend a lot a cash, and I suspect we'll be seeing quite a lot of each other." Then you have a deal. If you want to impress your mates or a frosty date, tip the doorman heavily so he remembers your name – always a power trip. The Arabs really know how to work a hotel: they tip every employee on arrival and the whole hotel dances to their tune.

Having established an intimate understanding, there are certain rules of engagement. Discretion is key. So it's best not to shout, "Can you score me some babes and blow" across the lobby; instead, mutter *sotto voce* when the coast is clear. Prostitutes are quaintly referred to as

'Prostitutes are quaintly referred to as "extra pillows" and are usually sourced through the concierge himself'

"extra pillows" and are usually sourced through the concierge himself (NB: if you skip the get-to-know stage, don't be surprised by a delivery of plump, duck-down pillows). In fact, it's only polite to go via the concierge for such services – they may throw out girls that guests have selected themselves. Prostitutes will be sent up to your room and drugs may be delivered by the bellboy or handed over by the shady character lingering at the bar – the concierge could never be seen to mediate such vices. The main thing

to remember, however, is not to be embarrassed. Whatever you want, he's seen it all before. Morning-after pills, vaginal douches and enema kits are all part and parcel of his remit.

It's worth noting that hotels will do anything to keep celebrities happy – that way the hotel gets to ride their publicity. If a coke orgy with 100 prostitutes is going to help them enjoy their stay, so be it (see How to Be a Star, page 126). The suite party – a celebrity favourite – is a very big deal in hotels, and as debauched as it gets. If, say, there are insufficient stocks of Krug, then of course it's fine to dispatch the concierge to all the clubs, bars and restaurants still open to buy them up. The rule of thumb in luxury hotels is: if you're spending enough money, you can behave how you want.❖

Live Like a High roller on a Lowlife Budget

By Simon Mills

Simon, a journalist and high roller, once travelled from New York to Nice on a privately chartered Concorde with 40 Victoria's Secret models for three days of partying at the Cannes film festival. His net worth is anybody's guess

TRUE STORY: in the late 1980s, a professional conman and Herculean hedonist decided that the quickest route to the fast-lane lifestyle of an F1 driver was simply to steal his identity. Posing as one of the slower, and therefore not so recognisable drivers on the grid, he went on a mammoth spending and fucking spree, procuring sports cars under the pretence of "testing" them… and then forgetting to return them. He seduced high-octane women and charged five-star hotel rooms to fake credit cards bearing the real driver's name. Eventually, after much international chicanery and pedal-to-the-metal partying, the bounder came to a sticky end after borrowing a £50,000 Lotus for a "photo shoot". A holidaying Lotus employee spotted the car outside a Marbella nightclub and alerted Interpol, who found our man in bed with a prostitute, in possession of a fistful of fraudulent credit cards.

Then there's the tale of Porfirio Rubirosa. You might not have heard of him, but really, you should be worshipping at his altar. Rubirosa was the Western world's last great playboy. He came from a poor Dominican family, but somehow managed to parlay his way into parties, princesses and panties all over the world. He raced at Le Mans, played polo and hardly worked a day in his life. "Work? It's impossible for me to work," he once said. "I just don't have the time!"

How did he do it? Well, for one thing, Rubirosa had a massive dick. "Rubberhosa", they used to call him. But he was rich beyond the trouser department. Millionaires and movie stars wanted Rubirosa around because he was an absolute gas to be with.

This was no accident. Early in his career, Rubirosa came up with a 10-point plan to achieve a state of total hedonism. In his book, The Last

Playboy, the writer Shawn Levy explains how Rubi decided that he would need good clothes – handmade, preferably – and that he would become proficient in one sport – the more dangerous and expensive, the better. Languages would be useful for "blandishments" with foreign girls. To be a good dancer was essential, but you also needed some cash to get into casinos, bars, clubs and restaurants. Oh, and good taste. And so on.

The point is, heavy-duty hedonism is hard work. If you weren't born into money and can't be bothered to earn it legitimately, it's going to take some low-level graft to be a high roller. Plus bits of wisdom from both Rubirosa and our Lotus joyrider. Without getting caught, of course.

The general rule for pay-as-you-go playboys is to act like a big shot when on show, live like a pauper otherwise, offsetting your bargain-basement missions with high-rolling add-ons. So, fly budget to Nice, then take the helicopter shuttle to downtown Monte Carlo. Once there, eat like Henry VIII on someone else's tab and starve yourself for the rest of the time; stay in the cheapest hotel room to save your cash for the most happening beach club.

Try and paint a picture of slightly mysterious independent means. Act like you belong, not like you are delirious with excitement. For instance, never, ever queue at nightclubs. Call ahead and get on the guest list. Your millionaire pal will be amazed at such cunning because his answer is to throw money at everything.

As a house guest at a rich friend's Ibizan villa, you must sing for your supper and sustain Olympic stamina. "The least sign of ordinary sloth or boredom or complacence could be a crushing turn-off," warned Rubirosa. The rich can behave as badly as they like. You, however, will always be under scrutiny. Bring a present and pretty girls, fuss over your host's kids and write thank-you letters; don't Bogart the coke mirror. Be generous when you can, grateful when you can't. You can't pay for the speedboat to the beach restaurant, so pay for cocktails when you get there. If in doubt, think showbusiness – imagine yourself as the entertainment.

Never brag about the money you have or don't have. Only jerks do that. Above all, don't be a fantasist, like our fast-lane friend. Don't lie about your education and your career. The rich are often rich because they are smart. You'll be caught out in a second. Try to be more Tom Ford than Tom Ripley, and you could be the next Porfirio Rubirosa.❖

James Muldowney

Wing it with Jets, Boats and Hookers

By Oscar Humphries

Oscar is a sometime writer and full-time 'playa'

BUDGET AIRLINES ARE a giant advertisement for going private. On a recent flight from Athens to London, I returned a pen I'd borrowed from the male "customer-service representative" (flight attendant). He took it back and said: "Thanks m'love." The nerve of it. The sheer Big-Brother-entitlement, we-are-all-equal cheek of the man, who looked about 12, but at the same time like he'd been around the block a few hundred times. Sitting next to screaming babies or very large, very fragrant bearded men also makes me long for my own jet.

> **❝You can do whatever you want on a private jet – except fly it into the Houses of Parliament❞**

However, private jets, even with the arrival of "affordable" VLJs (very light jets – do keep up), remain out of reach. I've never chartered a plane and would like to think that even if I had hedge-fund cash, I would, um… care enough about the environment not to use one. But I flew to Milan on a friend's jet once. As one does. It had eight seats, cashmere blankets and a loo. No queues, no naff airport shops selling Tom Clancy and Danielle Steel, no groups of young men in rugby shirts with "The Sperminator" and "Muff Eater" slogans. But, more than that, I loved that I could smoke on the plane. There was also a small dog onboard. You can do whatever you want on a private jet – except fly it into the Houses of Parliament. You could have sex on a private plane! I didn't because of the dog and the altitude and the fact that my travelling companion was 50 and tipsy. Next time.

You know what they say, if it flies, floats or fucks… get someone else to rent it and then charm your way to a free seat. If you are pretty, available and spend enough time in Tramps, Crystal or the lobby of the Dorchester hotel, someone will eventually insist that you come to St

Tropez with him and his friend Akbar. This ticket is not free, and payment is likely to involve both Akbar and Amir and a very large, potentially painful bottle of Dom.

Start a thread on Asmallworld.net about how you really need to get home to Nice because you've just broken up with your boyfriend. Post this in August and someone is sure to come to your rescue with a G4 or similar. Boys are less likely to get "free" lifts, but there must be the odd oligarch or sheik who likes a bit of sausage, so shop around.

If you manage to get on a private plane, go wild. Smoke. Bring your dog. Try and have sex. If you smoke a lot, then the cabin will be hazy and this will be easier to conceal. Remember to take pictures of yourself onboard to use on your Facebook profile.

Boats
Turn up in a port with a serious yacht and you will never want for friends – boats are a magnet for the socially ambitious. Tourists will ask if they can photograph your boat – you can always ask to photograph them back (especially if they are young and attractive). But no matter how large or lavish, yachts are always claustrophobic. If your host wants to listen to the Gipsy Kings at 3am, then you'll be involuntarily tapping your foot to Volare with them. If they want to leave the shores of Cap Ferrat for Sardinia, there is nothing much you can do about it. The idea of bobbing along the Riviera, chasing Russian hookers who think that I am "less than dog", is about as appealing as spending an evening with friends who go on about how much money they've made in property. Still, if you must, there are ways…

The Med is solid with boats in the summer, cruising like turds from port to port. Stand on the dock looking fine for long enough and someone will ask you onboard. Again, this is not an invitation without strings.

As with jets, it's trickier for the boys: your best bet is signing up as a crew member for the season. You'll be on the boat, but you will be serving the caviar, not eating it. Ogling the young girls from the Ukraine, not…

Be careful what you wish for. Boats are lusty places and squidgy things happen when you mix booze with Arabs on a jolly and fast-moving tide. Two miles offshore, nobody – least of all the man who gave you the Ecstasy – can hear you scream.❖

A Hedonist's Guide to Decadent Travel

By Nick Bornoff

Nick, the author of Pink Samurai, "an erotic exploration of Japanese society", and more mundane guidebooks, is prone to nostalgia about sinful journeys past

"SEX", THE FILM historian Donald Richie once avowed, "makes the ideal souvenir." To be properly decadent, your journey should entail sex and drugs. Seek out the rapidly shrinking realm of the "unspoilt" and spend your time and money astutely after dark. Don't vomit in resorts or do fish and chips in Spain. Decadence is pleasure with "clarse". For true escapism, flee into the minds of our romantic forebears. Think of a trip an intelligent ne'er-do-well might have taken during the golden age of travel.

Seducing his way around Europe, Casanova was probably the greatest archetype for travelling decadents. Barely a generation after his death in 1798, wanderlust swept the continent as the Grand Tour became the precursor to the gap year. The more decadent British grand tourists included Byron and Shelley. Ah, misbehaviour in foreign climes!

Is this possible today? Maybe. You need to be something of an aesthete and unabashedly fond of exotica; you must also match an intrepid nature with ruthless self-indulgence. Balance them carefully, however. Too much of one will jeopardise the other. And while you may be just another tourist, you don't want to look like one. You need a dress code – the city is not the beach. Avoid straw hats (and anything sold in souvenir shops). No pith helmets. Grubby white suits look good under overhead fans.

"Thou hast the keys of Paradise, oh just, subtle, and mighty opium!" so opined the 19th-century intellectual and addict extraordinaire Thomas de Quincey, who never actually needed to leave Britain for his fix. But drugs were high on the agenda with Orientalism. Tottering around Egypt and Turkey in the 1840s were Parisian literary figures – among them Théophile Gautier, Gérard de Nerval and Gustave Flaubert

Celine Clanet/Getty Images

– almost the entire membership of the naughty Club des Haschischins (yes, that is hashish) in Paris, minus Baudelaire, who was probably too far gone to travel.

Narco-tourism is still possible today, but most destinations are too dangerous to visit or under draconian drug enforcement (it's sobering that 16 Asian nations inflict the death penalty for cultivation and trafficking). You'll always find drugs where there's a shit-hole brimming with violence and eye-rolling fanatics. Proceed with caution! Never buy off the street; the product might be catnip or talcum powder, and the peddler a policeman (see page 74 for more tips). Check out the hippy hangouts first. Some countries offer opportunities to visit tribal peoples – select those cultivating poppies, cannabis or cocaine, and don't lose sleep over your anthropological interest sinking to the ethnological equivalent of dressing up porn as art. You should be too stoned to care.

One expeditionist who always put dissipation first was the early 20th-century gadabout Aleister Crowley: poet, writer, certified drug-sponge and peerless weirdo. An ostensible mystic and Satanist, Crowley founded a sex cult in remote Sicily (though these days, you'd need to go a lot farther afield). Maligned by moralists and loving it, he was something of a beatnik pioneer.

Indeed, look to the beats, those avid post-war prophets who showed the hippies the way. Some (Alan Watts, Gary Snyder) dug Buddhism and green tea (beneath Japan's austere façade, sex sizzles sempiternally), while Allen Ginsburg, Jack Kerouac and the profligate William Burroughs fulfilled all their needs – carnal, alcoholic, narcotic – in Tangier, Morocco. A consummate globetrotter, Burroughs was perhaps a paradigm for decadence abroad. Though don't, as he did, go playing William Tell with a wine glass and a loaded revolver, and shoot your wife in the head at a dinner party in Mexico City.

When it comes to "souvenir" hunting, hopefully you'll want whores, not slaves. In the bars, brothels or streets, talk to the girls. If they look bewildered or miserable, go elsewhere. Most speak enough English to tell you what's on the menu. BJ on the rocks, anybody? Fellatio with ice cubes is an old Manila favourite.

Avoid prison, especially in the developing world (too late? See page 182). Some South American jails offer five-star hotel sojourns with hot and cold running whores if you can afford it; if you can't, you suffer the same sordid treatment as everyone else. If deterred by travellers' tales of being beaten and bum-fucked by third-world police, you could just settle for a pilgrimage in bygone travellers' footsteps. The El Muniria Hotel in Tangier, patronised by Burroughs and the beats (and where The Naked Lunch was writ) is still there, but it's now a boutique hotel. Take heart, however. Decadent travel paradises are out there. When you find them, just don't tell. Otherwise, someone will populate them with package tourists, and someone else will make them illegal.❖

How to Pick a Horse in a Paddock

By Sir Clement Freud

Sir Clement, who is related to most other Freuds, will not be 100 for 17 years and has owned racehorses for most of his life. He would not still be working had they run faster

THIS ESSAY CONTAINS INFORMATION THAT COULD LEAD TO BANKRUPTCY.

Gambling, then – there is but one rule. If you mind losing money more than you enjoy winning it, keep away – play solitaire, move to Bognor Regis, whatever. I have always believed that betting within your limits is wholly pointless. To spend time, energy and intellectual capacity working out which horse/dog/athlete is going to come first and then backing your opinion with insufficient ammunition to realise the price of a case of decent champagne is pathetic. As Milton wrote: "High heaven rejects the lore of nicely calculated less or more." What you must do is plunge. Feel real pain when selection is stuffed so that you can rejoice at the magnitude of your win.

Let us now concentrate on making money at a racecourse. Avoid information. Owners do not know – quite apart from paying to purchase a thoroughbred, the enormous training costs, entrance fees and transport bills tend to make them wildly optimistic. They are also ignorant of the form of the other horses. Trainers won't say, unless you are the owner and owe them a lot of money, and jockeys are scared shitless, lest what they tell you is deemed to be "insider information" and they get sent to jail – where there are many other jockeys. Newspaper tipsters are not a bad source because if they fail to give the odd winner, they lose their jobs and have to start working. If a professional tipster suggests a horse that appears to have no chance on form, his pin could have got stuck in the wrong column, or he might, just might, know something.

There are those who bet because of the horse's name, the colour of the silks worn by the jockey, the number on the saddlecloth. If that goes with being at odds of less than 33-1, coming from a reasonably successful yard and being ridden by an in-form jockey, then there's no reason why not. Don't change your mind – absolutely nobody wants to know that you nearly backed the winner.

If you go to a racecourse, it is a bit pointless to sit in the restaurant and watch the action on the TV screen behind the bar. You can do that at home, where you are likely to eat better food and sip less expensive drinks. Before each race, visit the parade ring and look at the horses as they are led around, mounted and then cantered to the start. They mostly look alike, until you examine them with care. Some are grey, others range between dark brown and light chestnut, and many have blazes of white on their faces or legs. None of this has anything to do with how they run.

Some have larger feet than others. As a general rule, if the going is very soft, such as after a lot of rain, a horse with small feet will not do well. As the trainer knows this, he would not have entered the brute unless he/she is an exception to the rule. You will see horses that appear to limp. Although a horse that walks well also runs well, there are plenty who wait for the start of a race before they show noticeable enthusiasm for anything.

Very fat horses – said to show a lot of "condition" – are best avoided. In a sprint race, go for the one that has the biggest bum as long as he looks well (shiny coat) and the stable-lad/lass manifests an aura of cheerfulness.

Make your selection and bet with whichever bookmaker gives the longest odds (a substantial bet on the Tote, unless at a big meeting, is likely to depress the dividend). An elementary knowledge of maths is necessary here: 11-10, 6-5, 5-4, and 11-8 may all be available somewhere. Smart folk take the 11-8.

The sure way to come home poor is to have the same bet on every race. Vary your stakes: £500 (which in racing is called "a monkey") on one race and then a proper heavy bet on another in respect of which you feel more strongly. Back to win, not each way (which means first, second or third) if the odds are 10-1 or less. Don't bet to win money – bet to fly first class to Las Vegas and stay at Wynn Hotel, or to buy a large white truffle or a gold watch with platinum hands and diamond movement. When you lose, modify your expenditure for a while, like a few nights of dinner at McDonald's or Nando's.❖

Cameron Spencer/Getty Images

Poker Skills for Life

By Eliza Burnett

Eliza, the author of Girls' Guide to Poker and editor of
Poker Europa magazine, plays online under the pseudonym
Busybody – if you dare

I CAN LOOK a priest in the eye and lie with the ease of a politician.
The better you can lie (and call lies), the more money you make on the
poker table. It's all about mastering the bluff – deliberately deceiving
others into believing you're holding a stronger hand than you really are.
And the tricks that win on the felt work in life. Not something to tell
small children, perhaps, but true. Honest.

Consider this applied poker: to bluff successfully is to win that job
with an embellished CV, to seduce with a rented Ferrari, to get
upgraded because you look expensive. Likewise, to see through bluffs in
the sport of life is to outfox deceitful lovers, disingenuous estate agents
and even used car salesmen. What's more, the rewards aren't just
external – they bring a rush of blood to the head. It feels as good to
catch a bluff as it does to execute one. That's why dirty rotten
scoundrels the world over are at it.

The key is in cold-reading (and concealing your own) "tells", those
telltale signs that reveal all is not as it seems. Try this experiment: ask
a friend 10 questions – they must answer truthfully. Watch their eye
movement. Then ask them 10 more, telling them to lie in one answer, at
which point their eyes will involuntarily move in a different way. You
now have a tell on them for life. Tells may be as obvious as shaky hands
and pounding chests, or subtle, such as repetitive betting patterns and
excessive chatting while bluffing. With practice, you'll spot the most
notional squirm. It's a poker myth that tells are confined to dilated
pupils. I'd be happy for all players to wear sunglasses as long as they
continue to shake, gulp and avert direct questions (remember to watch

for these tells in your own game). In fact, wearing shades can blind you to your opponents' tells, and in life, a determined attachment to them will arouse suspicion.

On the other side, being a crack bluffer is all about control, requiring resolute conviction and a cool temperament. Convincing your opponents depends on your table image and the frequency of your bluffs. When betting, you need to maintain exactly the same pitch of voice and body language as the last time you raised with a strong hand. It's not as easy as it sounds. Note that a "rock" (a tight player who plays only premium hands – easy to spot as they don't get involved) is more likely to claim a pot without being challenged than a "fish" (a loose player who plays lots of hands hoping to get lucky and outdraw the rock).

> ❛It's a poker myth that tells are confined to dilated pupils. I'd be happy for all players to wear sunglasses as long as they continue to shake, gulp and avert direct questions❜

Success is dependent on not only knowing how to bluff but when. By default, the chance of being dealt a good hand is rare (as indeed with life). Bet or raise as much as you did the last time you entered a hand, be it good or bad (so opponents can't deduce anything from your bet size), and re-enact the same body language and poise as when holding a strong hand. Sometimes a small bet works, because it implies that you want to be "called" as your hand is so strong – usually opponents fold, reluctant to donate yet more to your bounty. Equally, a huge or "all-in" bluff can work because it implies that you have such a strong hand, you're willing to risk all. Beware, though: in poker circles, we say the all-in bluff "works every time but the last".

Stress in poker equals bad poker. If agitated by a run of bad luck, step away from the table – or situation – and collect your thoughts. Body language comes flooding out under stress. Decisiveness, as opposed to dithering, is key. As the song goes: "Know when to hold 'em and know when to fold 'em."

Women (outnumbered by 50-1 in poker) always have their "helpless female" side to summon when required. It's your right to manipulate opponents' prejudices: I've had men "check" me rather than "raise" me to keep me at the table, and even slide poker chips in my direction. Such feminine wiles will also help you to get a more honest quote

Mø Tørhed

from a plumber or electrician.

The point is, don't fret about the hand you've been dealt, because it's all about the way you play it. Take a gamble. Like Kipling once wrote: "If you can make one heap of all your winnings, and risk it all on one turn of pitch-and-toss… then yours is the earth." ❖

Gambling Is Good for You

By Michael Holden

Michael is a writer based in East London. If he
really knew anything about gambling, he'd be living
somewhere else, doing something very different

AS I SIT down to write this, today's newspaper headline reads: "Court
told of gang's motive for £53m robbery." It may seem that explaining
the allure of gambling might be equally unnecessary, were it not for the
fact that robbery is a pursuit for those who intend to get away with it,
whereas gambling – in its purest form – is about one's willingness to
surrender.

To give up responsibility for our future to an external system of
control (in this case luck), whether it exists or not, is a form of freedom.
What's more, it is a form of freedom made noble by the fact that it
persists in the absence of others – hence the popularity of gambling in
jail. In the act of betting, the gambler is abdicated from the regular
mechanics of existence. Elsewhere, we are encouraged to abide by the
notion that broadly speaking, we get what we give. Either that, or we
plod along in stoic surrender to the hand that life has dealt us, seldom
daring to try and bluff our way out. Social compliance is balanced on
the understanding that, despite what advertising tells us, we can't really
have everything, and certainly not all at once. The real slogan of
modernity is "Don't Just Do It", to which gambling, in all its forms, is
sometimes the only sensible riposte.

As gamblers, we come unstuck only when desperation or ego
intercedes and we start seriously expecting to win. Shakespeare nails it
when Macbeth grasps for a moment the possibilities of fortune – "If
chance will have me king, why, chance may crown me" – only to try
and fight his way to the top instead, and fail. Such are the dynamics of
tragedy, the professional gambler understands that in the long run,
dramatic outcomes are about something more complex than pure will.

The degenerate gambler is encouraged by imagined gradients in their own fortune. The reason it gets a bad name is because persistent gambling can bring out the degenerate in almost anybody. But then it wouldn't be gambling if there weren't any risks.

The thoughtful gambler understands that they are probably doomed and flutters anyway – and in that respect, gambling is exactly like life. It was Jeffrey Bernard – the bibulous British journalist who was never one to kowtow to the rationale of self-preservation – who pointed out in one of his essays on horseracing that "in most betting shops you will see three windows marked 'Bet Here', but only one with the legend 'Pay Out'". It was his prerogative to know the odds and reckon a life without betting a far worse proposition. He died without much money and in a ruinous physical condition, but he was sustained by the fact that right up until the end, he was making his own decisions.

It would be remiss to consider gambling without some mention of its earthly capital, the city of Las Vegas. A gaudy spectacle, perhaps, but consider which idea is really more offensive: a million people feeding money into machines in defiance of daylight, or billions of us pretending that life itself is not a perverse gamble, that there is some logic at the heart of it and if we just hang in there and pay our taxes, everything will be all right? When we contemplate the random nature of what shapes our lives, we prefer to dress it up as destiny or justice, but these are nothing more than luck by another name. In Vegas, people are in tune with the infinite in ways that religious communities can only dream of. Just because most of them are wearing polyester tracksuits doesn't make it any less so.

In the same way that sex is not simply a matter of having children, or drinking a question of thirst, gambling is about much more than winning or losing. It is about kicking against the flow, regardless of the outcome. There are nobler struggles, but they are not nearly so easily available. It's said that fortune favours the brave, which might seem unfair of fortune, given that the brave already have bravery on their side, but it is precisely fortune's unfairness that has made gambling – one of our most ancient vices – everything it is today. If life were fair, we would have given up on gambling long ago.❖

Hedonism in the Home

By Jenny Éclair

Jenny, a stand-up comic and novelist, is 47, which is – unfortunately – closer to 60 than 30. These days, she likes 'an early night'

THE TROUBLE WITH being an ageing hedonist is that hedonism starts to hurt – it gets you round the back of your neck and on particularly bad days, it leaves you dry retching, barely able to stand, the corneas of your eyes peeling away with dehydration.

The lily-livered among us would take these physical manifestations as a sign to give up and join a book club – and, may I just say, there is nothing wrong with joining a book club, as long as you only read filth. The rest of us have reinvented a new style of hedonism for the middle-aged, with the accompanying motto: "Keep hedonism in the home [it's cheaper and you're less likely to be arrested]."

For starters, I don't go out drinking any more – what's the point? You pay silly money for poor-quality booze, which you are then required to drink standing up while some idiot DJ in a stupid hat plays something you've never heard before at a zillion decibels into your ears. What's more, you are surrounded by younger, prettier versions of what you used to look like before you got fat and bitter and all the thread veins burst around your nose.

Why put yourself through all that mental and financial torture when you can drink indoors? I love drinking at home. It's marvellous: none of that worrying about getting back or forgetting where you live because you're already there, in front of the telly, in a towelling robe. Towelling robes are great – they're like an all-in-one nappy, soaking up any dribbles or spills. Recently, I have been toying with the idea of decanting alcohol into a baby's bottle so that I can just lie on my back guzzling.

I can't tell you how much money I've saved by not going out because I've had to replace the carpet several times, but I do know that buying booze online is cheaper, more efficient and a lot less

Model: Nina Kate
Jan Schjetne/diggetydamn.com

embarrassing than having to explain to the girl in the off-licence that, "No, I'm not having a party."

Another great plus about keeping hedonism in the home is that "home" is the only place left where you can smoke. The fact that I gave up 18 months ago is irrelevant; pretending that I can't face the pub because of the smoking ban is a great excuse never to buy another round again. Obviously, with the fags (and, incidentally, the narcotics) being a thing of the past, I've had to find other things to do with my hands. Masturbation is fine, but it's very upsetting for the window cleaner and, like anything, can get monotonous. So what other hobbies can the non-knitting home hedonist take up? Eating is good. I never used to bother much when I was smoking and taking amphetamines, but it's amazing how much enjoyment a middle-aged hedonist can get simply by stuffing one's face. Biscuits are really nice and there are all sorts of different types and flavours, so it's possible to be quite adventurous. Try a garibaldi dunked in a gin and tonic, or absinthe and a custard cream – really, I can't understand why anybody is still doing cocaine.

> **'Recently I have been toying with the idea of decanting alcohol into a baby's bottle so that I can just lie on my back guzzling'**

Writing letters to the council about collecting your rubbish is another domestic hedonist's thrill. Now this sounds duller than it actually is, but I promise, you can really get off on it. I've got a stationery fetish anyway, so writing anonymous poison-pen letters to the council in green ink with a special pointy nib can almost bring me to the point of orgasm.

Talking of which, sex tends to go a bit out of the window as you get older – this is the problem with having been very promiscuous in the past, you sort of run out of fucks. You've only got so many, and once you've wasted most of them, you've got to ration the rest for special occasions like Christmas and birthdays.

The fact is, you might not be getting much action, but other people will be, so remember that you can always live vicariously. If you have children old enough to be sexually active, read their diaries. It's almost as much fun as doing it yourself, and you don't need to wash the sheets.

So there you go, your complete guide to keeping hedonism in the home. Why bother going out when you can cause trouble in your own house and spare yourself those embarrassing court appearances? ❖

The Cucumber's Guide to Cool

By Tom Stubbs

Tom is an ambassador for deluded pillocks everywhere

NIETZSCHE PROPOSED THE idea of living life as art, saying it was the only way "to transcend life's absurdity". Our version is living life as cool, no matter what. Rule one, there are no rules to being cool. You can go your own way. Don't get hung up on the traditions of cool – the true rubric also flows in counter-eddies and backwaters. Try new stuff, try old stuff, try what you like. Not caring ranks highly. Telegraph nonchalance and you're on the right road.

Never fall in love. Unless it's with someone you've only met twice, then let it melt quietly inside your chest like a discarded ice-cream cone, without ever telling anybody. And never hold hands with someone you're seeing. Especially not in public.

Approach your life as if making an art-house film of yourself. Musical backdrops, atmospheric wide shots, close-ups, silences and bouts of inspired self-expression. Difficult, of course, but we can't all be cool, after all. Cool is what you do in those unscripted, uncontrollable moments that define you; when you meet yourself in the eye of the storm as the severest of life tests rages all around. A well-delivered line stays with your spirit forever.

Embrace your inner pillock. Get your head around your foolish tendencies and foibles, and make them part of your modus operandi, ie a fondness for sweet sherry, despite being a Hells Angel. Cool is about conviction – an unswerving confidence in your home-made elf costume as you bowl down Main Street will leave pretenders and lightweights stunned and open-mouthed in your wake.

Apply wit whenever possible. Even kings and queens of cool have to do rubbish and unglamorous things. Like, say, poo-ing or having an operation. Can you poo cool? No, and nor can they. When you're in a hospital smock waiting for the needle and the knife, consider your last words before you go under. They could be your last, so make them dry and sardonic. For a laugh, why not have a dig at the anaesthetist? They laugh, you laugh, and your backless nightie and paper pants are momentarily forgotten. Apply cool reactions to all hideous embarrassments. It's pretty exhilarating, actually. Savour rubbish moments – this way, you can never get caught out.

Be liberally nonchalant. For example, you get a call from the top boss. You enter his office, where he's waiting with your line manager, both looking sheepish but resolute. You're gonna get it for sure, so you might as well be cool and make the bastards squirm. Make yourself laugh, while setting up some memories to cherish for life. "Hello. You both look tense. What's up?" Then later, "All I want to know is will I still be able to attend the Christmas fancy-dress parties?" Watch them answer with confused sincerity – and relief – that of course you can still come. Ha. Like you'd want to.

Financial privilege and beauty are handy, but they're certainly not a fast track to cool. Of course, there's a load of stuff that's inherently cool, like sunglasses and swearing. But it's what you do next that's key. Fashionable and trendy aren't cool ideals. Base your look on cult film characters and personalities (Ferry, Bowie, Morrissey, McQueen and Eastwood are all worth noting), and make sure everyone knows. But knowledge (on any matter, not least Nietzsche) doesn't make you cool. Processing stuff as and when does. So, don't say too much about specifics – it might sound like showing off, which isn't cool. Fake your look with a personal shopper if desperate, but beware of studied cool. We can all see through that. A few embellishments, such as a hand-appliquéd watch-strap depicting Jarvis Cocker's stage invasion at the Brits, might be just the frisson your look needs. And never say anything is the best. It's only gonna get as good as okay – even if you're raving inside, never give above a seven.

Meet and greet with earnest and unaffected pleasantness, only to demonstrate far more affection to your real friends. Chat like you're enjoying yourself, but also like you're conducting an undercover exposé in your head. Always have several agendas running parallel – that way you'll never come across too keen. Don't bother to strive to remember people; if they're not engaging enough, that's their problem. This is life, not an entrance exam to the Natural History Museum or the neighbourhood-watch scheme.❖

6

Trouble

❝ Anything's legal as long as you don't get caught ❞

The Traveling Wilburys

Opposite: The Norwegian Way Jorn Tømter

How to Gatecrash

By Nicholas Allan

Nicholas, author of the children's book The Queen's
Knickers, and the grown-ups' book The Complete Guide
to Gatecrashing, has crashed more than 2,130 events,
at one of which he shared a 20-minute conversation with
HM Queen Elizabeth II about her underwear

ARE YOU POLITE, attentive, high-spirited on demand, a good
listener, able to take on others' problems? If so, then you have the
makings of a gatecrasher. You need only two other accessories – a
black Armani outfit and unflinching amorality. Gatecrashing is one of
the last criminal acts (a cocktail of theft, fraud and confidence trickery)
still unvisited by the legal profession. And the greater the risk, the
greater the pleasure, as any city trader, serial killer or bondage
practitioner knows. Like all great disciplines, it must learnt.

Lesson 1: The nursery slope – the art gallery private view (PV)
Amble through a city's art gallery locale during PV primetime, 6-8pm.
What you're looking for, of course, is food and booze. What you must
look like is someone who doesn't need to look for food and booze.
When you find your target, amble right on in, proceeding directly to
the paintings – refuse the cheap wine, refuse the canapés. Suspicion
deflected, you can now get rat-arsed in your own time. Art,
incidentally, gives you the opportunity to speak to strangers without
fear of perverse intent. You can then glean information about other
PVs down the road.

Lesson 2: Private parties at large hotels and restaurants
Eventually, you will achieve PPPP – Psychic Precognition of Possible
Parties – but in the meantime, hotels and restaurants are your training
ground. Conceal about your person a champagne glass. Arrive during
peak congestion. Loiter. Then, after a flurry of guest activity round the

Stranger (©2006) courtesy of Foley Gallery, NY / Thomas Barry Fine Arts, MN
Thomas Allen

door, approach, with mobile in one hand, glass in the other. Beam at the doorman, say jubilantly, "It's a boy!" and skip smartly by.

Lesson 3: The red carpet party

Two ways in: ingeniously subtle or crassly blatant, both high risk.

Method A: Walk up the red carpet towards the uniformed thug with the clipboard. As he searches for your name, select one that you see on his list (preferably, as much as you can be certain, the same sex as yourself), say, Sir Richard Basingstoke.

"Your name doesn't seem to be here, sir."

"Eh? Oh, maybe they've used my real, rather than professional, name."

"And what would that be, sir?"

"Basingstoke. Dick Basingstoke."

"Enjoy the party, sir."

Method B: Wear a showbiz dress or black tie, with shades; borrow or even hire a car and driver and a glamorous partner – you'll only need them for five minutes for 500 yards. Circle the drop-off point and wait for your decoy – a star. As the star is ambushed by photographers, follow them in. Make straight for the loo to remove the sweat from your face.

Once in, amuse yourself – and be a good guest – by talking to the celebrities of your choice. This requires previous homework – swot up online on lesser-known details of invited celebrities, for instance, Rod Stewart's model train-set collection. Used wisely, your arcane knowledge will fascinate and flatter them into prolonged conversation. Remember, politeness, like your Armani, even at a punk-rock reunion, will always be respected, because both are associated with cash. So, it is not "Johnny". It is "Mr Depp". NB: never forget your goody bag. It's often worth more on eBay than all the booze and food you consume. (Say your partner couldn't make it and take two.)

Lesson 4: The full five-course dinner with accompanying wines
The Ritz, the Hilton and other "luxury" establishments are your standard hunting ground. You already have your invite for the pre-prandial reception – a black bow tie in your inside breast pocket and a BYO champagne glass. Wait until you are called to dinner, then go to the loo. When you return, you'll easily find your designated seat – the empty one. (A law of gatecrashing is that for every 50 dinner guests invited, one will be infinitely delayed, ill or dead, sometimes all three in very rapid succession.) "Would you mind?" you say. "For some reason they've put me next to my wife. Who, tomorrow, I should add, at crippling expense and litigation, will be my ex-wife."

Have You Passed?
You'll know when you've reached the Zen state of liggerdom. In the post comes an invitation to a prestigious social event. You've actually been invited. But it's not surprising. Your social skills as a seasoned gatecrasher make you the person any host would most like to see at their party. However, if the ligger-bug has entered your system, your heart will involuntarily sink. This invite has ruined any conceivable kind of fun you might have had. You've no choice. You bin it.❖

Breaking the Law for a Laugh

By Martin Deeson

Martin, a journalist and GQ columnist, has –
like everyone else – broken the law many
times, sometimes just for a laugh, sometimes
just because it was there

FROM WHAT I'VE seen of the world's police cells, there are few
things more antithetical to pleasure than waking up behind bars with
a thumping hangover, a cold pit of fear in the stomach and a Scottish
tramp. This fate must be avoided.

Of the six or seven times I have ended up in the clink, at least five
of them were in Hackney in 1990. It was the year of behaving stupidly.
Hackney was the perfect place to rebel against your background, drink
Special Brew, do speed and bemoan the fact that daddy couldn't afford
to buy you a squat. Of course, I could have got a job in the City if it
weren't for the class war sweeping backwards and forth across
Thatcher's Britain. That and the four ear studs, and the can of Special
Brew and spliff welded to my arms like prosthetic hands.

And so, the police – quite reasonably – started arresting me. First
there was possession of weed, then fare evasion, then climbing over a
wall with a crowbar to turn a derelict building into a squat, then things
got a little more serious, with a pull for possession of
methamphetamine and finally culminating in a few days in Dublin
prison for the diametric opposite of the perfect crime – stealing a
CCTV camera.

Waking up in police cells in London is bad enough. Waking up in
prison in a (then) hostile foreign country is very, very scary indeed.
I realised I was shit at crime. So I developed a few basic survival
techniques to avoid being the muppet singing, "I fought the law and
the law won." What sounds passable as a white reggae lyric is utterly

unamusing when staring at six blokes doing smack in a prison wing run by the IRA, going, "And who the feck are you?"

And so, my five tips for enjoying crime are:

1. **Do not get caught**
Obvious really, but I wish someone had told me this when I was 22.

2. **Go for deniable crimes**
When on planes, kneel over the toilet bowl, light a fag, and, holding each drag in for the maximum amount of time possible, exhale over the toilet whilst simultaneously pressing the flush button so the suction extracts all the smoke. When the stewardess knocks on the door, say: "I'm glad you've come – this loo positively reeks of fags." Then barge past her with all the confidence that a man who's drunk seven children's-sized bottles of wine can muster. Which is a lot.

3. **Never nick what you can't afford**
Once you have a department store bag in your hand, you are on a licence to graze. Build up confidence in the food hall: take a hefty selection of food up to the coffee shop, sit down and proceed to eat. Then procure a couple of magazines (folded under the arm, who wouldn't forget to pay for them?) and then get going on the stuff that it would only be human to pop into your bag without paying for: expensive pens, overpriced greetings cards, fancy books. In fact, anywhere capitalism is taking the piss is fair game: motorway service stations, for instance. Just fill a tray with food, sit down and start eating – it'll take an eager wage slave indeed to interfere.

4. **Do not feel guilty**
All property is theft. Probably. Capitalism is built on the exploitation of the… Oh, whatever. Look, they're bigger than you, they're probably American and they make loads of money while you have trouble paying your phone bill. If you must worry about thieving then always do it from faceless corporations. Obviously, to run off from your local Italian restaurant would be both immoral and stupid. To run off from the breakfast buffet at an international hotel, or to sign your whole breakfast to an entirely fictional room number is actually making a blow for the oppressed Mexicans who clean the rooms, somehow.

David Waldorf/Getty Images

Would Che Guevara admit how much he'd had from the mini bar when he checked out? Don't be daft. He'd just shout "Cuba Libre!" and run off.

5. Think!

If you run from a cab fare going, "I'll just nip into this tower block and get the money," then they will go back to the friend's house you booked a cab from. I apologise to all my friends I've done this to.

Finally, if it all goes tits up, don't phone your lawyer, phone your agent. There's always room for another My Prison Hell book. At least I hope there is… ❖

Freeloaders Will Save the World

By Fleur Britten

Fleur retired her wallet back in 1989

CONSIDER A MOMENT the oceans... Picture those cleaning stations where small "cleaner fish" tenderly groom larger, grubbier fish. Without these marine drive-thrus, the big fish would surely plummet to the ocean bed with the sheer weight of their excess baggage (and the cleaner fish would certainly have to skip a meal or two). Instead, both species live happily ever after in mutual benefit.

Back on land, the freeloader provides a similarly noble housekeeping service by mopping up the excesses of conspicuous consumption, nibbling away at that filthy lucre. There's way too much to go round in the Western glut, and the planet is burning under the burden. For those who cannot turn down the volume on their spending, the freeloader is here to help – yes, help – those who just can't help themselves. At million-pound parties where champagne is showered like confetti, half-empty Nebuchadnezzar bottles become ashtrays and herds' worth of Kobe beef are left uneaten as appetites mysteriously disappear into the night, up steps the trusty freeloader to save the world from itself.

Like life in the oceans, this party's for everyone. The big spenders get off on largesse and the chance to display their have-it-all status, while the freeloader not only gets a kick out of something for nothing, but, by doing their bit for wealth redistribution and landfill management, gets to bask in the glow of a much bigger, more selfless ideology.

We're not suggesting bin-diving for food past its sell-by date with the rats and the freegans. Freeloading is much more fun. For starters, there are all those bloated, big-budget parties begging for your service. No need for invites – much better to crash it (see How to Gatecrash, page 158), then you're unaccounted for, and thus not part of the problem. Aim straight for the VIP suite for the drink, drug and goody-bag mountains.

Then there are Nice Friends' Houses. But not just any old nice friend:

Miko Miroslav Vranic

they must be pre-enlightenment, ie those who have (or aspire to) a fleet of 4x4s, champagne baths, remote-control curtains etc. Be prepared to provide payback, be it in charm, gossip or sex, but never feel ashamed – it's you doing them and their bin guilt a favour. Plus they like the attention. While there, invite yourself to forage through their only-wear-once wardrobe and, if feeling really militant, start squatting. At least get a doggy bag.

More advanced circles partake in mutual freeloading, where it is possible to exist almost money-free (though, annoyingly, with the trade-off of moral superiority and bling comedy value). Get yourself into a barter system with friends: muck in with a farmer, a brewer, a chemist and a chocolatier to cover all your basic needs. There is also the kindness of strangers to harvest. Cropping up in cities are car shares (posh hitching), swap shops and freecycle groups, where "offereds" and "wanteds" fuel a virtuous circle of sharing and re-homing. You might even make new friends to cadge dinner off.

But the most needy causes of all are businesses, just crying out for your benevolence. It has always been the (perverse) case that the richer you become, the more freebies you get. Now, with the advent of citizen journalism and reality stardom (see How to Be a Star, page 126), access to a quite disgusting array of perks has never been more democratic. Establish yourself as a freelance journalist or cult blogger and stem the vast leakage of cash that is publicity. But while you could (very) easily call in a shipment of beauty products, daily hampers, and a lifetime's supply of music, books and <insert favourite ice cream here>, actually, you can't, because then you'd just be causing more expenditure, and not – so the argument goes – making money go further.

> **❛There are always spare seats going in first class, and all that gourmet cuisine to rescue from a wasted life and a lonely death❜**

The cleanest freebies are things that are happening anyway – gigs, films, sporting events and so on. And designer fashion: save those pretty publicity blondes from the sack by borrowing clothes and giving them exposure. There are always spare seats going in first class, and all that gourmet cuisine to rescue from a wasted life and a lonely death. Seduce the check-in attendant, "slip a disc", be "on your honeymoon". The same goes for hotel upgrades – yours to blag.

By all means say thank you for all that you receive, but never, ever say sorry. Freeloading is philanthropy… on your part. By cleaning up the spills of profligacy, you are fixing matters beyond the comprehension of the benighted, all the while stoically tolerating the vulgarity of their look-at-me cash-splashing. Only not spending shows real taste. The buck stops here.❖

Skive for a Salary

By Tom Hodgkinson

Tom Hodgkinson is editor and founder of The Idler,
author of How to Be Idle and an expert in idleness

SKIVING IS THE reassertion of dignity in the workplace. It is a way
of grabbing back time for yourself from those to whom you have
foolishly sold it. That crafty fag by the bins, the slow stroll back after
being sent out on an errand, that lingering in the loo, that half pint in
the pub at 4pm: these are the delicious pleasures that skiving affords.
Skiving adds zest to life; it is, in fact, living.

And in this age of regulation and surveillance in the workplace, we
need more than ever to develop our own skiving techniques. Long
gone are the 1970s, the golden age for skivers, when the unions
institutionalised skiving in the form of proper lunch hours and tea
breaks. These periods of time out were sacrosanct; they were part of
the deal: "Okay, we will work for you and your giant enterprises, but
don't think about working us too hard." Now that old culture has all but
died out. Unions are weak – we have to be strong for ourselves.

First, you need to adopt the philosophy that pleasure is good and
therefore skiving is good. To avoid unhappiness, stress and resentment,
we need to fill our days with pleasure. Unhappiness comes from a
dearth of pleasure and a sense of powerlessness. Therefore, you owe it
to yourself and your health to enjoy life.

Hard work is for the stupid. Only slavish morons work hard for the
company. In the old days, we were not so obsessed with work. The
medieval peasant worked fewer hours a week than we do. And
overwork was frowned upon by the clerics, since it was seen as
indicating a lack of faith in God's providence. You were supposed to let
things happen rather than take the arrogant step of attempting to
control your own destiny. "Consider the lilies of the field," said Christ

in the Sermon on the Mount. "They toil not, neither do they spin."

So, armed with the knowledge that skiving is good, you can now go ahead and do it without guilt.

The two most important activities that work disrupts are sleeping and drinking. Neither seems to be approved of by bosses, though both are crucial ingredients of a well-lived life. Napping techniques must be developed. I heard of one worker who perfected the art of napping in a toilet cubicle. He would sit across the loo with the seat down, his legs jammed against one wall and his head cradled by the loo roll. I used to take forty winks at my desk, my elbow on the table and my hand propping up my chin. And I hear that sleeping supine under a desk passes quite convincingly as Alexander Technique practice. Alternatively, seek out quiet spots near the office: the park bench or the church pew. Take a nice fluffy pillow with you, preferably scented with lavender.

As for drinking, you must drink more. Take at least one pint or glass of wine at lunchtime. Instead of forking out on industrially made sandwiches, bring your own and buy a bottle of champagne with a co-worker to drink in the park. Delicious! Apart from being a pleasure in itself, a little light drinking at 1pm will take the edge off those gloomy hours between two and four, and can also be argued away as "team-building" and "creativity-cocooning".

Then you can always fit in a quick half at teatime. Just pop out to the loo, keep walking, go to the pub, drink and return. Nobody will be any the wiser. Because you have enjoyed your day so much, you will not feel the need to rush out on the dot. Hang around for a bit and make yourself look keen to the boss. (Warning: not too keen, as this is impolite to your co-workers. Nobody likes a try-hard.)

Everyone should know how to pull a sickie, another great British tradition. The best excuse I ever heard was "problems at home". Nobody is going to press you on that one. And when you are genuinely ill, for heaven's sake don't self-medicate and work on through it. Stay in bed for three days. Skiving is power. Skiving is liberty. You have a duty to do it. ❖

In Praise of Protests

By Dan Kieran

Dan, author of I Fought the Law, has organised a cricket match for the 'Ashes' of the Magna Carta outside the Houses of Parliament, walked 30 miles along the Thames to Downing Street on a freedom pilgrimage and held an illegal teddy bears' picnic by Westminster Abbey, all in the name of protest

PROTESTS ARE GOOD for you. First, it's shouting therapy, as pent-up tension is exorcised in short, sharp barks. Then there are all those like-minded new friends to be had. But most importantly, protests are good for you because they're good for your rights. The only way to get what you want is to demand it: "What do we want?! When do we want it?!"

So, how to make your voice heard?

First, find a cause that makes your blood boil. Happily, for the modern activist, there are plenty of gripes to choose from. Not least freedom of speech itself. You can now be arrested for holding a political demonstration outside the Houses of Parliament, unless you have permission from the police. I met a man convicted for holding a banner in Parliament Square that read: "If you do not believe in freedom of speech for people you despise, then you do not believe in it at all." For the rest of his life, whenever he applies for a job, he will have to answer "yes" to the question, "Do you have a criminal record?" and deal with all the prejudice that this implies.

Or how about the fact that you can now be arrested for doing literally anything at all? The police used to have three crime parameters: there was the non-arrestable offence (cycing on the pavement etc), the arrestable offence (shoplifting etc) and the serious arrestable offence (assault, fraud, burglary, rape etc). But our government decided that these terms were too confusing for the police, so they just made "anything" an arrestable offence instead. Not only that, under the Prevention of Terrorism Act 2005, you can be imprisoned without trial – so much for the presumption of innocence.

Then there's the fact that anybody arrested gets their DNA taken, along with fingerprints and mug shots, regardless of whether they've been convicted. Britain has the largest DNA database in the world (with 5% of the population on file; in second place is Austria, hardly a bastion of progressive political opinion, but they only have 1% on theirs). Our database even has samples from more than 50,000 children who have never been found guilty. And in Britain, we have the highest number of CCTV cameras per person than anywhere else in the world. Brave New World meets 1984, anybody?

But if that's too frightening to tackle, there are plenty of daft laws to complain about. Take the Sex Offences Act 2003. This masterful piece of legislation makes it illegal to have sex in a public toilet. So if you were thinking of it, then for goodness' sake, don't. Just have sex up against the outside wall of the toilet instead – perfectly fine, according to the law.

If you don't live in the UK, then you might not think any of this matters to you. But Britain is the cradle of western democracy. I asked Prasanth Visweswaran, the "criminal" who held that banner, why he was prepared to flout the law. He replied: "Because this is Britain! Britain is supposed to be the gold standard of democracy. It's more important to fight about it happening here than anywhere else." Like it or not, if these kinds of policies take hold here, it's only a matter of time before they spread across the globe.

So, with blood duly boiling, it's time to take to the streets. But how best to fight for your rights? Your audience is your first consideration – what better way to reach millions than by making the news? However, some silly publicity stunt is unlikely to have the world's news networks tripping over you. No, your best chance is by being the sideshow at something they're already covering: offer a bit of excitement during a lull in the sporting/ceremonial/royal action. You need to be both media-friendly (gimmicks, nudity, celebrity names – yes, the media is that shallow) and people-friendly, because attracting a crowd attracts hype fast (try bribing bystanders with a tot of brandy, and bring enough for yourself).

Your protest has to be a performance – think sensory overload. There are tried-and-tested strategies: for instance, the Raging Grannies, radical cheerleading, pretend-handcuffing to railings, die-ins (fake deaths on pavements; require liberal use of stage blood, otherwise they can resemble a sleep-in). But nothing startles like real

Make Poverty History, Edinburgh Bruno Vincent/Getty Images

shock can, and this is your aim. But whatever you do, just don't get overexcited and turn violent – bad publicity will crush your cause. And do something rather than nothing, because everyone else is far too busy working and shopping to care. And you'd better do it quickly or we're all screwed. ❖

Blag Your Way Backstage

By Moby

Moby, a musician, has spent much time backstage, both invited and uninvited. More often than not, he is nonplussed by how dull backstage experiences tend to be

THERE'S A COMMON misperception that the backstage area of a rock concert is a utopia of hedonism and debauchery, and that going there will rank alongside graduation/virginity-loss/bar mitzvah as being worthy of deathbed remembrance. The sad truth is that backstage at almost any rock show is a relatively mundane and/or a sad place populated by sweaty roadies, sleepy truck drivers and hungover musicians trying to find a place to lie down or throw up.

However, enough rumours have grown into legends to justify a bit of hype. Kate Moss supposedly shagged Har Mar Superstar while Kings of Leon looked on backstage at one of their gigs; Jimmy Page apparently had a fondness for transvestites and underage girls, and always travelled with a whip… Er, I rest my case. At least there's outrageous riders to be entertained by – like Van Halen's famous insistence on no brown M&Ms anywhere in the backstage area, the Smiths demanding a tree "more than 3ft high", Mariah Carey saying, "I don't do stairs."

> **'Once at the venue, the key to gaining entrance is to look bored and mildly purposeful'**

However, also contrary to common belief, it's surprisingly easy to get backstage (another urban myth, not least thanks to Robbie Williams, who sang in Rock DJ about roadies only giving out backstage passes for blow jobs: "No head, no backstage pass."). The first and easiest way is to go online and find out about the backstage pass (or "laminate") artwork for the band you're interested in stalking. Any fan site will probably have examples of artwork or, alternatively, you can go on

Backstage at the Barfly Muir Vidler

eBay and buy a backstage pass for about £5. Find a clever friend who knows how to use Photoshop and have them recreate the pass. Then get it laminated, find some string with which to hang it around your neck, put on butch black roadie clothes and get to the venue early (ideally 3-4pm).

Once at the venue, the key to gaining entrance is to look bored and mildly purposeful. Walk through the backstage entrance, possibly giving a perfunctory greeting to the security person manning the door. Maybe even ask them a peremptory question, like, "Hey, where's catering?" Then you're in. And once you're in the venue, you're really in. The only quasi-restricted area is the artist's dressing room. Everywhere else is open to you. And if anybody asks what you're doing there, say "local catering" or "picking up lighting" or something totally trivial and unworthy of challenge.

So now you want to meet the band. Catering is the best place to do this. Hang around long enough and eventually the band will come in. Nobody pays attention to the catering area – you can hang out for hours, drinking coffee and reading newspapers, and nobody will hassle you, and eventually your rock-star heroes will arrive for dinner or coffee or a happy little bowl of cereal.

Another advantage of getting into the venue early is that you can watch sound-check, when the musicians run through their songs to make sure that the equipment is working. If you're in the venue during sound-check, you can, essentially, hang out wherever you like and hear your favourite rock gods perform desultory versions of your favourite songs. If your goal is rather to sneak into the after-show party, then you have different options: a) be a stunningly attractive woman and ask the tour manager where the after-show party is, or b) pretend you're from a local radio station. Then make friends with the least popular member of the band or one of the hired musicians. The lead singer gets all the attention and is the most jaded, whereas the drummer is usually relatively friendless – he will happily respond to your queries and will most likely tell you where to find the after-show party.

And remember, the key to your success is to follow the advice of Obi-Wan Kenobi and use the force. If you believe that you're supposed to be backstage, then you shall be backstage, and nobody shall attempt to throw you out. Have fun and enjoy the free luncheon meats on the deli platter.❖

How to Be a Rock'n'roll Rebel

By Miranda Sawyer

Miranda is a journalist who has interviewed
several real-life rock'n'roll rebels, including
Johnny Rotten, Shaun Ryder, Noel Gallagher
and Ozzy Osbourne

OKAY, CHAPS, ARE you sitting comfortably? Well, stop it immediately.
Nothing about the rock'n'roll rebel should ever feel easy, body language
included, so please slope to the nearest vertical surface and assume the
correct position. Back against the wall, eyes scrunched, fag lit, one foot
tapping, one hand in pocket. Not the hand with the cigarette.

Better still, leave the room altogether. Rock'n'roll rebels are mostly
myth, and the best way to bolster your legend is never to be there.
Make them wait. How long, naturally, depends on who they are. Male
friends can be left to stew for about three hours, as long as you keep
updating them with promises of free blags into a dodgy shebeen/posh
bird's house party. Females? A week, at least. Parents? All year, except
on their birthdays, when you should return to the family home for
lunch, hair flattened and nails clean, bearing plastic-wrapped flowers
bought from the garage. Music journalists? Half an hour tops and then
apologise with meaningful intensity while giving them the Full Bambi
through your fringe.

Oh, sorry, you're not actually *in* a band, are you? Not to worry.
Attaining rock'n'roll rebel status is often quicker without the loser
extras, such as band members or songs. Though you should have some
form of creative outlet: art, writing or music. You need to be
misunderstood, and you can't be if there's nothing about you other than
that cat-scaring haircut to puzzle over. As rebs are meant to be cleverer
than mere mortals, you're best off if your "work" isn't too concrete, and
therefore open to criticism. Diaries should be scribbled scraps of paper;
songs, strummed chords with improvised words about whichever girl
you're singing them to. Art must be extravagant and free-spirited, but

sabotaged, either with smeared blood, or by you smashing up the canvas in a fit of aesthetic dummy-spitting.

What else? Don't eat. If you're anything heftier than a size double zero, get yourself a heroin habit. Don't sleep. Don't sit in the sun. You're channelling Byron, not Beckham. And don't wash. Okay, maybe a damp flannel wiped around the dangly bits is only polite (ask your dog), but never let cleansing products near your jeans or your hair.

Perhaps you're thinking that this all sounds a bit too much like hard work. If so, may I remind you of the numerous benefits of being a rock'n'roll rebel. First, and most importantly, you get the girls. All of 'em, from fit to frump. And their mums. Maybe simultaneously. Second, you get the good times. If you follow these instructions, then sex, drugs and rock'n'roll will become your constant buddies. Along with all those who like their company.

In fact, if you're not a people person, then really, this job isn't for you. Despite the moody appearance, the reb is a gregarious soul. So get out there. Pick a social whirl (tip: go super-swank or utterly skanky – there's no such thing as a suburban rock'n'roll rebel). Once in your chosen milieu, pose like mad, but cultivate your cheeky chat. Say the unsayable, especially if it's rude. A great technique is to describe what's actually going on in any given social situation. No matter if a person is irritated, horny, drunk or random, if they're trying to hide their feelings, point them out to the general company. It breaks tension – well, it causes fights – and it makes you look clever and outrageous: vital traits. (There are those who would have you believe that rebels don't talk. They're stuck in the Marlon Brando past. Your modern-day icons are Pete Doherty and Russell Brand, and you'd have to pay those two to shut up, as Kate Moss probably knows.)

If you had to sum up the appeal of today's rock'n'roll rebel, it is this. Look scary, but be as friendly as a lost labrador. It's unbelievably disarming. But, if you choose this route, don't wimp out. No matter how charming and affable, the rock'n'roll rebel should always be out for himself. So harden your heart. Shine your light on the young, the vulnerable. Get them hammered, introduce them to some tawdry practice (shoplifting, crack, anal sex) that they've never dared try before. Have your wicked way. Call them at ridiculous hours for a few weeks. Then stop. Withdraw your love. Wipe your memory as you wipe your dick. And the day you hit 35, give up, you sad git.❖

Top: New York Dolls, Spain 2007. Above: Brixton 2007 Irene Barros

How to Sweet Talk the Cops

By Tom Stubbs

Tom, a writer and stylist, was once a very
well-behaved schoolteacher's son

THERE ARE TWO circumstances in which you can find yourself at the mercy of the police. Innocent or guilty. Degrees of both vary, but either way, you want out of that enfeebled position fast. Compliance is key. The more swiftly you communicate your wholehearted willingness to comply in all lines of inquiry, the better.

Policemen like power. Be it to compensate for their own perceived lack of it, or perhaps some embarrassing Freudian inadequacy, or simply because they are genuine do-gooders, they crave control like a drug. So make it easy on yourself – indulge their power appetite. Don't begrudge this act of servitude, they're begging to be respected – liked, even – so give them it all. Keeping schtum once collared will just antagonise angry powermongers. Curse and detest later, when you're skipping about freely.

First, address them as "Officer" without the slightest tick of resentment. And let them know you appreciate their good work. "I respect you for stopping me and investigating, Officer. Thank goodness someone is doing their job." The Old Bill loves to point out others' stupidity: "Thank you for identifying my mistake, Officer. I shall take heed." Be sincere, they'll lap it up.

Now relax and enjoy the grilling. The "these aren't the droids you're looking for" Jedi mind trick is unlikely to work, but the theory is the same. You're simply not the droid they're after. Achieve this by exhibiting comfort in the hot seat. Maintain pleasant eye contact, your brain working happily and steadily behind clear eyes.

Then there's the method act. If you have done something badly wrong, have a decoy scenario vividly in place. Use old emotions and sensations like a method actor would. You may well have 56 pre-wrapped grams of coke strapped to the inside of your pants, but concentrate, say, on having just taken your old mum out for a nice Italian, and how you both got a little tiddly. Think of pleasant, innocent stuff and hold onto it when interrogated. If Dibble looks puzzled or unconvinced, push further: she really does get stuck into a glass or two of Sancerre, and sorry if you're tipsy. He'll probably think you a foolish, rambling softy, but not a criminal. Don't insult a copper's intelligence by telling over-the-top lies. Do give him the chance to feel like a good chap by letting you off your minor discrepancy. Give him the option of being magnanimous.

An earnest confession of a sensitive nature will help buffer any lies you're about to tell. Work on a personal level, such as admitting you were upset about being dumped, and now appear drunk and have nearly wee'd yourself. Or, if caught urinating behind the post office, play the ex-boyfriend card, saying he broke your heart and worked there. Cry a bit. Works for boys and girls. The police aren't that good with gays on the whole.

Other sexual prejudices can be manipulated, too. Driving with a loopy girlfriend the morning after a stiff party, I went the wrong way down a motorway sliproad. The first car I passed was Motorway Patrol. They had me park up on the verge by the biggest No Entry sign in Cornwall. "WHAT ARE YOU DOING?" he asked sternly through the window with utter disbelief. I shook my head and asked to be interviewed in the privacy of their car. I composed myself, but let slip some discomfort for their benefit. "I'm really sorry, Officer, but she was just going on and on and on, and it was driving me mad. You know how women can be sometimes? In the end I just took the next left to shut her up. You must understand, it was relentless..." The plods smiled knowingly at each other. They didn't even breathalyse me. Apparently, they did understand.

Using a fake disabled badge to park illegally? Try this line: claim to have just helped out a twisted old invalid who, out of gratitude, offered to take you to lunch nearby. You parked here as he offered the use of his parking-exemption card. Now you wonder, to your dismay, if he might not be all that he seemed, as he's vanished, leaving you in this terrible predicament. "What on earth can we do now, Officer? Would a description help?"

The short and long of it is to avoid taking the Fifth Amendment and follow the 11th Commandment: "Thou shall not get caught." Obviously. But we are weak. So play ball, be grateful, and you shall walk free again shortly. As you were.❖

The Norwegian Way Jørn Tomter

A Hedonist's Guide to Prison Survival

By Howard Marks

Howard has spent well over 3,000 days in a total of 15 prisons in America, Holland, Spain, Hong Kong and the UK

YOU ARE LIGHT years from home with no friend, family or fellow countryman anywhere around. You are confined within a small area surrounded by razor wire fences, electric fences, searchlights and patrolling uniformed psychopaths itching to use their machine guns. Your fellow inmates are assassins, urban guerrillas, child molesters, serial killers, cannibals, rapists, mass murderers, snitches and other perverts whose pleasure derives from others' pain. You are physically weak and skint. You are a smart arse with a degree and several kids. You are attractive and all the other male prisoners fancy you. You have no choice of food, clothing, employment, bedtime, waking-up time, work time, interior decoration or roommate. You have no television, radio, sound system, computer, telephone or sight of a female body. You have no drugs. You are on your own in the belly of the beast. You are buried alive.

The absence of your family will tear your heart out. Nobody can wait for you that long. You will witness gang rape, garrotings with guitar strings, stabbings of vital organs, attempted decapitation and 200-strong free-for-alls in which the participants slice each other up with home-made swords, kitchen knives and sheets of glass. But don't worry. You will become numb and impassive to all forms of blood, guts, hysteria and grief. You will also get ill. Smoke and phlegm will fill your lungs and an ill-fitting denture plate will dangle from your mouth. How are you going to survive, motherfucker?

Realise you are almost completely forgotten When banged up for a long stretch, you're a complete pain in the arse to everyone outside. Nobody knows what to write or send. Life is much easier for them if they forget you. Don't take it personally.

Don't take yourself too seriously Even in the free world, you have no meaningful control over events. You are insignificant. In prison, this is ever more the case. You can't control what happens to you, but – and this is so important – you can totally control your attitude to whatever is happening.

Never show your fear Animals smell fear and go for the kill to get their food. Humans smell fear and go for the kill for their money, pride and sexual pleasure. Never show fear.

Keep fit One way of getting even with the bastards who put you away is to have the same life expectancy on your day of release as on your day of arrest. Another is to escape by scaling fences, jumping gun towers and disarming prison officers. Both require dedicated preparation and a certain level of fitness.

However, prisons do not really go in for the transformation of an unhealthy, confused and possibly feeble delinquent into a fit, powerful man, focused on revenge against the system that destroyed everything he had. There are no gymnasia. Prison cells, however, are ideal for the practice of yoga, the oldest system in the world of combined mind and body development. The basic postures, asanas, are a series of strange but surprisingly easy-to-learn positions that keep the body lean and flexible. The practice stretches and tones every part of the body, and through twisting and turning, massages the internal organs. I'm not going to rave on about inner peace. Quite simply, the exercises make sense: stretching and breathing, as opposed to contracting and puffing, and overcoming the physical discomfort generated by some asanas gives a sweet, calming feeling. I don't think it's the least bit necessary to avoid chemical highs, but it's comforting to realise there are other ways of achieving similar mental states.

Always help people Resolve firmly to assist the inhabitants of your immediate environment. It's easy, and there's no downside.

Don't give up the fight The bastards would dearly love you to rot in prison. You feel you can't win. There's no way out. That's not a good enough reason to stop fighting. The way of the warrior is correct, win or lose.

Don't grass The only guaranteed way I could avoid a lifetime in prison was to testify against my friends. And never, ever again be able to look my parents or kids in the eyes. I would have preferred to give up the ghost and lay down in the prison cemetery, the graveyard of those forgotten before they die, than to grass.❖

Clean(ish) highs

'The last time I opened my chakra
so I could feel my peace,
I got thrown right out of the pub'

Anonymous

A Teetotaller's Guide to Hedonism

By Will Storr

Will, a journalist, spent his school years getting into hedonism-related trouble with almost everyone and left with no qualifications in 1993. He saw his first therapist in 1994. He became teetotal in 2003. His first book, Will Storr Versus the Supernatural, was published in 2006

THE FIRST TIME I got drunk, I was alone. Twelve years old, sat upstairs with a stolen cup of cider – just one sip made me want to spin with my arms out and giggle. What I remember most about that moment is how much it frightened me. One mouthful and I was transformed. Electrified. Up in the air. The gabble of anxious voices in my head suddenly coalesced into a single one – a brand new version of me that was confident, joyful and fierce. As the happy danger spread warmly up my body, I knew. This was too nice to be anything good, too powerful to be holy. I poured the rest of the fizzing potion into the bathroom sink and watched it disappear down the plughole like a hissing serpent. That night, I had a revelation from the most primitive depths of my brain. It gave me a terrible feeling, like that split second when you realise you're about to fall out of a tree but haven't yet started the tumble. I knew that hedonism was going to possess me. It would piss its brilliant evil all over me and I'd have to drag myself, shivering, out of its reach. It was inevitable that one day I'd become teetotal. The truth is, some people simply aren't built for excess.

The folks that can take it are the blessed elite. They can spend a lost weekend sniffing coke and sucking cock, and then sashay into work on Monday looking as-cool-as and behaving as if it was all just a bit of a laugh. But for people like me, hedonism is terrifying – an infernal force – because it provides everything we need most in a form that couldn't be more dangerous for us. You see, we're the wonky ones; the bullied, the ugly, the Catholics. We're full of holes and, in our hopeless attempts to fill them, we crave love, attention and respite from anxiety. Hedonism provides: stimulants give us the confidence to talk, tease and act like those miraculous people we see on the telly. They enable us to negotiate dirty encounters in strange bedrooms and experience total acceptance in a concentrated dose.

But the problem is, we're not strong enough for it. When the amphetamines and gin release the pressure, we can't deal with the explosion. We can't be extroverted without hating ourselves later, we can't get drunk without crying or smashing up stuff, we can't have casual sex without falling in love. We need it all much too badly. We become tormented by fun.

And so, inevitably, we give it all up. But for all the pre-teetotallers out there, I have good news. That doesn't have to be the end of pleasure. The teetotal way has many quiet delights, all of which are deliberately kept hidden from those people still caught up in that noxious parade of spunk and shouting they call a social life. If you're planning on joining me and cleansing mind and blood for good, I have made a list of things you need to do:

1. Abandon the nightclub forever – it's nothing but a sticky box full of noise and cunts.

2. Truly, there's no fun like cheese-and-biscuits fun.

3. After 10.30pm, drinkers start repeating themselves. During these hours, pretend to listen while working on things in your head – sitcom ideas, bad poetry, murder fantasies, whatever…

4. If you're sober, idiots at parties will fear you. Use this to your advantage.

5. The "social lubrication" effect of stimulants is still enjoyable if you're sober. Simply wait until everyone's trashed and then, like an old person, start asking rude questions.

6. Bring a book to a restaurant and dine alone.

7. An electric blanket, a menopause-sized bar of Fruit & Nut and a Prime Suspect DVD, used together, produces a blissful, back-to-the womb buzz similar to heroin.

Mark Douet/Getty Images

8. The unspeakable truth: alcohol tastes disgusting, and history's most celebrated brewers, distillers and wine-makers are merely the men who've best mastered the trick of disguising it. Drink tea. You'll be the last to bed.

9. At chucking-out time, walk through the staggering clouds of booze-wounded idiots listening to mournful classical music on your iPod. It'll make you feel like Jesus (I recommend Festina Lente by Arvo Part or the Schindler's List soundtrack).

10. Never be afraid to bugger off. "This is shit. I'm going home," are usually the wisest words spoken at any party. And they're most often muttered by that prematurely aged, miserably enlightened person hiding from everyone in the corner. ❖

The Thrills of Guerrilla Gardening

By Richard Reynolds

Richard is the author of On Guerrilla Gardening and founder of Guerrillagardening.org, an internet resource for illicit cultivators worldwide. Since the day he could crawl, he has enjoyed getting mucky in mud

WALK DOWN A high street and guerrillas will ambush you. Che Guevara glares down from a million T-shirts, a guerrilla marketer pounces with shampoo sachets, guerrilla golf manuals pile high in the bargain bins. And by the roadside, there may be a colourful clump of flowers, albeit planted without permission. Guerrilla gardening is not just another G-thing. Like the original 19th-century Spanish guerrilla fighters, we are fighting for control of the landscape. Like them, we are sporadic and informal, resourceful and optimistic. Our enemy is not Napoleon, our enemy is the abuse and neglect of land, and we fight with forks and flowers, not guns. The only casualties are weeds and litter. This battle is a euphoric one, for not only is the annihilation of neglected space hugely fulfilling, but also by growing things, we get gardener's pleasure, something with which regular green-fingered non-combatants will be familiar. The day your first snowdrop wakes up, your towering sunflower bursts into bloom or you serve a bowl of home-grown lollo rosso is unquestionably delightful.

But why garden in a self-imposed cage when there is the world beyond your wall to transform? Plants look better in public – nature's beauty should be shared. The sight of pedestrians slowing their stride to take in your work is the guerrilla gardener's ultimate reward. Besides, some of us do not have the choice, stuck in high-rise flats with not even a windowsill. Outside, the waste ground is a no-man's land of opportunity – public land! Make it yours and bequeath your blooms to all.

Is it illegal? On private land it is trespassing, but we want to give plants maximum exposure, so do it in public space – though here it could officially count as vandalism or an obstruction of the right of way. You can seek permission, but it is far simpler and more satisfying

Jason Morris

not to bother, and you are unlikely to be stopped unless doing something obviously obstructive and dangerous. There is no need for alibis and excuses – most people are blinded by the reasonableness of it.

Start simple. Some troops guerrilla garden solely with a handful of seeds and a screwdriver. In Amsterdam, a woman who goes by the name of the Ground Hog plants hollyhocks, prodding them into muddy crevices and next to tramlines. For two years, the Brussels Farmers have planted thousands of sunflowers around their capital. Late-night missions have turned the city golden, and the Oz-like jaunts along Brussels' yellow roads have become legendary after they survived a confrontation with the Wicked Witch of the West – they strayed too close to the American Embassy and were pounced upon by armed guards. Learn from their lesson and leave patches tatty if in jumpy locations. The thrill of a confrontation with a confused official is, for some guerrillas, however, part of the appeal.

And not only is there the satisfaction of turning eyesores into beauty spots, but these battles are often social events. Troops bring fighting spirit, home-made cake and sometimes even new dates (I suppose a late-night dig, with troops packed into a dark space working up a sweat, a heady aroma, a loud, urban soundtrack… It's like a dancefloor).

Nor is the solo guerrilla gardener ever alone – the curious will always stop. Anybody who dares approach a stranger wielding a sharp instrument late at night has something entertaining about them – typically busybodies, drunks and vicars. Their anxiety turns to joy when you explain that you are not stealing plants (concerned police did once stop me about this, but let me continue "stealing" chickweed), but simply making their neighbourhood more attractive. Sometimes they join in, return with a tray of tea or even press cash into your muddy hands. Word gets around. Now drivers cheer us on, making countless requests for us to do their gardens. And for some reason, cabbies seem preoccupied with why we are not wearing gorilla outfits.

It's not all a bed of roses. In subsequent weeks, you'll lose some plants and you'll learn a lot about your neighbourhood from litter (cider and ready-salted crisps are popular in my street), but on a sunny day, you will walk through your peaceful idyll, take in the vista and glow from the inside out. There is a thrill knowing that you created this; it is a magical moment, and you will beam like a giant sunflower. Plus you'll be high on all that oxygen.❖

How to Get Out of Your Head on Yoga

By Tony Marcus

Tony is a debased hack turned clean-living writer of repute, thanks to his obsessive yoga habit

RATHER LIKE COITUS, yoga usually finishes on a high. The yoga high is a floaty, blissful feeling indeed, not unlike *la petite mort* or even, though we would not recommend such a damnably corrupting habit, the alleged pleasures of marijuana.

Fortunately it is not necessary to engage in yoga's more strenuous forms to meet this high. The reader is encouraged to sneak a foretaste by perhaps lying on their back in a quiet, clean room and regulating their breathing – so perhaps they inhale through the nose for five counts and exhale, also through the nose, for the same amount of time. Once the breath is regulated, we would advise a raising of the knees, and then, in time, while the feet remain on the floor, that the small of the back is gently raised and lowered in accord with the movement of breath. As underwhelming as such activities may seem compared to the pleasures of the gourmand or seasoned sexual libertine, they nevertheless provide the yogi (or yogini, in the case of a she) with the most ambrosial of mental and emotional states.

However, there is much to be said for attending a public class. Not least, we must confess, for the pleasure of seeing so many young ladies poured into the tightest, flimsiest and most revealing of outfits. Yoga is terribly popular with the weaker sex. Perhaps the ladies derive something of the long-lost pleasures of the boarding school, but for a crimson-blooded chap, the experience is akin to entering a secret harem – rather like being an undercover boy privy to the ladies' inner hearts.

A single fellow would be well advised to consider the yoga studio (or shala, as it is known) as potential hunting ground for courtship. Once one is rather good at yoga, the ladies will be most admiring of one's svelte, tanned and snake-like torso when it is squeezed into an athletic vest and made to execute the most daring twists and bends. There is also something to be said for the very prettiness of the yoga studio; usually a splendidly high, light space, something like an artist's studio but without the fumes of paint, tobacco and red wine. Instead, it is filled with the gentlest of incense, the rhythm of human breath and sometimes the most agreeably Eastern-styled chanting and song.

Yoga teachers are not beyond making physical contact with their students. As the teachers are usually *belles femmes* themselves, we can report many a happy moment when said lady teachers have moved or flattened the flesh of our buttocks (a common move designed to expose the bones at the base of the pelvis) or performed an "adjustment" by actually lying on top of one, effectively using their entire feminine bodyweight to squash one more effectively into the pose. Many teachers discourage suffering, but it is possible, if we are so inclined, to make a medieval rack from one's own body and meet the very limits of bearable pain. We often ensure our pose is sufficiently incorrect to invite the attentions of our beloved Queen of Pain. It is a delicate and complicit humiliation – and the more public the ordeal, the more delicious the humiliation. When she finally lets go, she lets her hands slide down our forearm into a caress and breathes: "Good boy."

The yoga class ends with a pleasing few minutes of lying around doing nothing, in the pose of the corpse, or *savasana*, as it is known in Sanskrit. If one is lucky, the teacher will gently massage one at this point, running her shapely hands over one's arms and legs and neck. It is, again, a most gratifying experience. It is by no means uncommon for the teacher to enter into sexual relations with a student, although the etiquette of dating one's yoga teacher is sufficiently complex as to require an entirely separate entry that should be dealt with in a later book.

There are other pleasurable benefits that derive from regular yoga practice. One becomes fitter and more spry. Also, over time, something of the more exotic yoga philosophy begins to sink in and one may experience the temporary loss of ego. This sounds alarming, but we can assure the reader that to escape the tyranny of the ego and its litany of "I want, I fear, I desire, I need" brings the most indescribable bliss. It is rather like escaping from the most appalling marriage even if one was, paradoxically (it may seem, at first) married to one's self. ❖

Vanessa Ellis/vanessaellis.com

The Selfish Benefits of Random Acts of Kindness

By Cynthia Parsons McDaniel

Cynthia is a New York-based writer who, after navigating the dangerous waters of the entertainment industry, has realised the urgent need for random acts of kindness

HELPING OLD DEARS across the road, throwing your coat over a puddle, paying for the person behind you in the queue – it's pure altruism, right? A selfless, non-transactional act, with no expectation to be written into the old dear's will, to be loved by the girl in exchange for her trashing your coat, to make lovely new friends... No, with random acts of kindness (RAK), the carrot, at most, is "thank you" – and even that's not a sure thing. The reward comes from inside – that warm fuzz, that pure, pride-swelling high that makes your heart sing with goodness and moral high ground. It's almost drug-like – more powerful than the recompense of cash, more encouraging than gratitude. How else could Mother Teresa and Florence Nightingale have appeared so beatific? This buzz of self-love ("I surprise myself how nice I am sometimes") calls into question the selflessness of altruism. There are yet more selfish benefits: you also get to join the lucky luck club – think of RAKs as karmic insurance. And it's excellent for your personal publicity: "Sorry I'm late. I got caught up helping a blind man carry his groceries home." But the best thing about RAKs is that they don't require a 273% commitment to kindness, just discrete instances. Want in on the loop of goodness, but don't want your coat wrecked? Here are some alternatives:

The Mercy Fuck Okay, so they've been dumped, or they can't get a date. It's up to you to instill some hope that they deserve love once again. Imagine yourself on a flight and the man next to you has been left by his wife for the neighbour. You must save this man from feeling like a complete loser. You motion to the stewardess to bring alcohol. Let him cry, then cuddle him, maybe a little frottage, and oops, there we go! But you have to make it look like his idea. Also, make sure you are untraceable afterwards – no exchange of digits or any mention of where you work – ideally, remain nameless. In any case, that's a turn-on to a total stranger, and for you, it's sex without strings. Besides, you've both always wanted mile-high club membership; you exercised a few muscles and raised your heartbeat a bit, so there are health benefits, too. And it does help pass the time on that long-haul flight.

House-sitting for the Wealthy To have someone at home with the lights on and music blaring is a huge favour on your part, by providing a burglar deterrent for the owner. First off, case the place: service all the appliances, turn over the engine of the Bentley to charge the battery, give their clothes an airing to scare away the moths. Perform a "concerned friend" investigation of their medicine cabinet, wine cellar and desk drawers. Only after this task can you invite dates round – there's nothing worse than a guest asking for a glass of wine and you not knowing where it's kept. And be sure to Polaroid everything before throwing a huge party.

The Starter Friend Model yourself as a goodwill ambassador in your city. Showing a newcomer around town is a nice way to show kindness. Be they even a friend of a friend of a friend (ie a total stranger), open your heart and your Rolodex to show them the best possible time. Your friend may trade you up for a Bigger Better Deal, but this could be your opportunity to meet hot new people in your own city; in fact, you should encourage the BBD, and then you get your network ladder, plus you get to rid yourself of them. You might even get invited to stay for free in their city one day. Maybe you'll even become real friends.

Mentoring Getting down with the kids reaps all manner of benefits: free fashion education and new catchphrases on tap, plus the opportunity to listen into conversations on cool new bands, clubs and all sorts of other zeit-things. And you get to play God: by orchestrating their lives, you get to create a whole little person. And when they're running a global conglomerate, you might want to get your offspring an internship. Or yourself a job. As the saying goes, be nice to people on your way up, because you meet them on your way down.❖

Another Countryside

By Bethan Cole

Bethan, a writer, grew up in Shrewsbury where
she put the camouflaging properties of the countryside
to good use as a teenage vice den

THE GREEN IS infinite. It's the saturated green of trees and fields and
grass after summer rain. The green of pure chlorophyll laced with
pearly dewdrops of ozonic freshness. You have to stand in the field and
let the green seep into your mind with the insidiousness of psychosis.
You must not make those careless comments that seem to destroy the
experience of the countryside, such as, "What a wonderful view!" or,
"Oh [sigh] look at that!" The appreciation must be silent to work.

The bucolic ether of the countryside was my womb. Actually, I like to
think I was a child of the land, but in fact, I grew up in a sprawling
suburban housing estate that numbered 6,000. The houses all had
windows like wide-open eyes brimming with tears. This distended
village was surrounded by fields, though, and so, perhaps misguidedly,
we saw ourselves as country people. We roamed through horsetail-
dotted meadows on summer days and during cold winters we spent our
centrally heated evenings suckling at the narrative teat of Laurie Lee.

So it was in attempting to escape this Lego-brick estate that I grew to
appreciate the pleasures of the countryside. I sometimes think that
these "pleasures" are learnt rather than instinctive – or imposed. As
children we went on "the Sunday walk", even if the wind was whipping
around our faces, bringing tears to our eyes and searing pain to our
little ears. My mother would try to modulate this experience with
exhortations like, "Fresh, isn't it?!" and "Breathe in that clean air!" as we
struggled through biting gales atop mountains, clutching our anoraks to
our ears. No, no, not for me, those prescribed pleasures of the
countryside – striding forth in cords and wellies and proclaiming about
the view. You can keep your country walks and your River Cottage
rustic idyll. I want random, less conscious moments of interaction.

Jason Morris

I want solitude and silence. I want joys that inveigle my mind as subtly as poisonous vapour.

I suppose my enlightened and deconditioned approach to arboreal ardour began some 20 years ago, when I was 14. I had escaped the suburban dystopia our family called home by going on a camping trip with three friends – one couple and one solitary male – to some nearby woods. They were all goths, and we spent most weekends sitting in one of their bedrooms smoking and listening to LPs by Gene Loves Jezebel, Southern Death Cult and Throbbing Gristle. But this particular weekend, we decided to explore the pleasures of the countryside. So off we went with six bottles of Thunderbird, several packets of Marlboro Red, two wraps of amphetamine sulphate and our tents. It was summer, and the grass where we pitched the tents was parched and brown.

Once we'd erected the tents, we gathered some twigs and started a fire with a plastic lighter. We smoked cigarette after cigarette and passed around the Thunderbird bottle. Cigarettes taste better outdoors and you don't have to sit in a welling cumulus of smoke after each puff. We got drunker. We rubbed amphetamine sulphate onto our gums. We felt omnipotent; sleek, sharp racing creatures sat in the middle of the boundless green. The couple disappeared into the tent and then we had sex, me and the single goth boy. I didn't really fancy him, he had strange coarse, curly hair and listened to the Cure. It was all hormones, speed and teenage nihilism. Sex proved to be better out of doors, too. I felt liberated – a convulsing part of the world, with the sky and the trees, rather than closeted away in the privacy of the bedroom.

❝**So off we went with six bottles of Thunderbird, several packets of Marlboro Red, two wraps of amphetamine sulphate and our tents**❞

As I lay there in the moonlight on the grass, trying to disregard this callow youth sucking on my neck like a clammy parasite, my heart racing, speeding off my head, in that moment, breathing in the green all around me, I could feel the infinite, I could appreciate the cleanness of the air, the freshness of oxygen, and I loved it. Suddenly I had clarity. After all those years of people trying to tell me what I should love about the countryside, I finally understood its freedoms and pleasures – the unexpected, unmediated moments that cannot be appreciated under order. I had found my own communion with nature. And this has guided me ever since.❖

Ten Steps to Freedom

By Tom Hodgkinson

Tom is editor and founder of The Idler
and author of How to Be Free

FREEDOM IS A state of mind. It consists of recognising that you are
already free, and that you yourself have created your own life situation.
This means that if you choose to, you can create for yourself a different
life situation. Man is condemned to be free, as Sartre said. Freedom
means taking total responsibility for your own life. Anyway, enough
philosophising. Here are my top tips for a life of liberty:

1. Quit your job If you have any negative feelings at all towards
your job, then it is time to quit. Quit now. Don't reflect, don't plan, don't
wait for the right moment, don't procrastinate. Just never go back to
that accursed office ever again. Beyond your job lies freedom. It is not
necessarily an easier life, but it will, at the very least, be a proper life –
your life – and not a slow death.

2. Play the ukulele The ukulele possesses four strings that could
change the world. The uke is very cheap and very cheerful. It's very
portable and very easy to play. After just a few months of strumming,
you will bring joy to the world and to yourself.

3. Stop voting When you put an X in a box, you are handing over
the responsibility for your life to a self-interested clique of bureaucratic
busybodies. We vote, we moan for five years, we vote again. And
politicians always, always disappoint, whatever their party. It's in their
make-up. Stop voting and start facing up to your own life. Make nothing
happen.

4. Dig the earth Gardening was one of the first forms of work
approved by the early Christian monks. They thought that work was a

vain activity and preferred contemplation, but made an exception when it came to gardening because it is creative, and God's work is creative. And it is wonderfully therapeutic to work with soil, and a miracle when the seeds you sow turn into something you can eat. Growing vegetables also releases you from dependence on evil supermarkets.

5. Disconnect Throw away your BlackBerry now, if you are unlucky enough to have been duped into buying one in the first place. The BlackBerry is an electronic manacle that promises freedom while actually taking it away by chaining you to the office. After that, disconnect more. Stop checking e-mails and stop reaching for the mouse every time you want to know the answer to a question. Replace technology with people.

6. Get on your bike If you want to be free, then stop relying on public transport and use your own two legs to get around. Cycling is a joyful experience because of the total liberty it brings. When on your bike, you control your speed, your route and how often you stop to gaze around. You also save a lot of money. And the lower your outgoings, the less you need to work.

7. Bake bread This is one of the easiest and most satisfying things you can do to look after yourself and improve your quality of life right here, right now. Buy a packet of flour, some yeast and a baking tin and you'll never eat factory rubbish again.

8. Cancel your direct debits My friend M said that direct debits are like making a little hole in the balloon of your bank account, through which others can place their grasping hand and take money out again and again. Direct debits are supposed to make our lives easier, but really they make more profits for Them, as we forget to cancel them when we cancel the service. Go back to cheques, or better, cash.

9. Do less Buy less, travel less, spend less, work less. It is man's tragic urge to interfere and to "do more" that creates life's fetters. The less you do, the less money you need and the more freedom you will have. Ecological damage is caused by doing. So by doing less, you will be saving the world and, more importantly, saving yourself.

James with ukulele Leonora Goddard and Gabby Laurent

10. Be merry Throw parties, bang drums, dance in the streets, get drunk often. The forces of puritanism have been cracking down on merry-making for 500 years, and it's time to reverse the trend. Music and convivial company will drive away your melancholy and ennui. We need to embrace pleasure without guilt. Pleasure is life: eat, drink and be merry. ❖

Cycling in the City

By Mary Wakefield

Mary Wakefield is assistant editor of The Spectator, and has a fancy bike and a death wish

TO DESCRIBE CYCLING in the city as a means of transport – even the best means of transport – isn't good enough. That's like calling skiing a way of getting from the top of a mountain to the bottom. Biking around a city is about harnessing the power of legs and cogs, honing judgments and risking death or awful maiming several times a day, just for the sheer pleasure of it. City cyclists are psyched, pumped full of adrenalin; it's why fist fights erupt at traffic lights and the air is as thick with swearing as it is with exhaust fumes. But we also have a secret brotherhood. We seek each other out at parties and settle down for hours to swap stories about head-first encounters with taxi doors, cracked collarbones and curb-smacked black eyes, all in full agreement that nothing will ever persuade us to take public transport again. For good bike chat at parties, try these:

Hop Like a Rabbit

Every city cyclist needs to know how to hop their front wheel up a steep curb at speed. Stand up on your pedals and lean back so that your weight isn't on the front tyre. Just before the curb, pull up on your handlebars and bump up onto the pavement. It's an essential manoeuvre for short cuts and for sudden shopping impulses. However, the rabbit hop will make you the sworn enemy of all pedestrians. For this you need…

The Zombie Stare

However slow you go, pedestrians – or Pavement People, especially Elderly Pavement People – will curse you with a violence and vigour that makes Mike Tyson look like Mika. Some may spit at you, others

Bike messenger, San Francisco 2007 Steve Newman/chefnewman@hotmail.com.

might lunge with walking sticks, aiming straight for your spokes. Don't be offended or afraid, just make like a zombie and stare blankly into the middle distance. On no account try to reason with a Pavement Person. Their rage knows no bounds.

The Hunt
Pavement People like nothing better than patrolling public parks in search of cyclists who've strayed from the designated cycle path. If they spot you, the race is on. They'll let out a great holler and begin running towards you, waving frantically. Under no circumstances must you stop. This is the city equivalent of fox hunting and your life is at stake. Move up a gear and keep pedalling until the yells are no longer audible. High speed is, after all, good for inducing adrenalin highs.

Stairs
Cycling down stairs is fun; it surprises pedestrians and confuses police. Practise on a short flight of shallow steps. Freewheel slowly towards the

edge and let yourself drop, keeping your weight back and only using your left, or back brake. Don't worry, you'll be just fine. And after that, there are stairs worldwide to be conquered: the long flight in front of the Metropolitan Museum in New York; the stone steps in Trafalgar Square in London; the Spanish Steps in Rome and, best of all, the 142-metre-long Potemkin Stairs leading down Primorsky Boulevard in Odessa straight into the Black Sea.

Hands Free

Unlike their more laidback country cousins, the city cyclist is a show-off. Even when the streets are deserted, they will still be performing for the pigeons. The first and most essential trick is learning to ride with no hands. Start by cycling around with just one hand, then, gradually, with a thumping heart, peel off the other. Soon you'll be swooping round corners with a mobile in one paw and a cup of hot coffee in the other. Remember, though, it's okay to drop the coffee in a life-or-death situation.

The Underworld

City underpasses and tunnels present a cyclist with the unique opportunity to experience the terror a small mammal must feel when chased by enormous, roaring predators. Lights on, if you've got them, straight back and then however frightening the motorbikes sound, make like Orpheus and don't look back.

Scylla and Charybdis

The sailors who passed between these two terrors of the ancient world must have known something of the fear and excitement felt by a city cyclist as they discover they are on the inside of a bus sandwich. And as you race through the narrowing gap between bumper and bollard, you risk being scraped to a thin paste on metal railings or flattened as a monster lorry makes an unexpected left. Even so, jumping the bus is the city cyclist's answer to shooting the tube on a surfboard. It takes nerve, judgment and skill. Just don't tell your mother. ❖

The Point of Pointlessness

By Sam Leith

Sam is literary editor of The Daily Telegraph, a job he regards as exquisitely pointless. People keep on buying Tony Parsons novels, whatever he tells them. And do they buy his own pointless book, Daddy, Is Timmy in Heaven Now? Do they buffalo

"THERE IS NOTHING better in life," according to the underappreciated pub-rock band Half-Man Half-Biscuit, "than writing on the sole of a slipper with a Biro/ On a Saturday night, instead of going to the pub." How very right they were. Claims have been made, by the literary critic Christopher Ricks, among others, for Bob Dylan's importance as a lyricist. But HMHB, as they are known to their relatively small band of devotees, seem to me to have pipped him here.

The slipper they were describing, of course, was that species of slipper, common in the 1980s, which had a horrible nylony upper and a rubberised sole the colour of too-milky tea. In his fine novel, The Mezzanine, the American writer Nicholson Baker talks about the intense pleasure to be derived from signing your name with a Biro on a credit-card slip at the supermarket, resting on the jerky, rubberised conveyor belt that has just conveyed your purchases to the till. He was describing exactly the same thing.

Scholars, philosophers, the adult and the sensible and the sane, priests, your mum and dad and probably Dylan will argue that writing on the sole of a slipper with a Biro is a pointless thing to do. But they will be missing the point: the point of the Biro, and the point of the pointlessness.

To take time out from your life – be it half a minute or half a lifetime – to do something completely pointless is the highest and most ravishing form of hedonism available. It is an act of existential heroism and, like, a total fuckin' treat. Think of it. You have only threescore years and 10, or whatever, of existing in this world. Some of this – years, according to the usual apocryphal statistics – will be spent asleep, or brushing your teeth, or telling people about your unsatisfactory weekend in Torbay. But some of it is yours. Why spend it finding out about the world, or sitting in a wretched pub attempting to make connections with other wretched human beings, playing darts, and buying double gin and lemons for people who will buy you singles back, and wasting their time and yours by telling them about your unsatisfactory weekend in Torbay?

All that will happen is that, in the short term, you will have a hangover and a faint sense of regret; in the medium term, you will die and forget everything that was said about Torbay or any other subject; and in the long term, the pub will shut and its doors will swing in the parched wind as post-human, Cormac McCarthy-esque cannibals make their way past its doors hullooing barbarically and pushing shopping trolleys full of tinned goods; and in the very long term, the sun will turn into a red giant, the earth will turn an interesting colour and not even bacteria will find it congenial any more.

Why not, then, spend the time available to you – purposely and exactly, and with calm deliberation – doing something that benefits nobody, that promises or claims nothing, that embraces futility? And yet something that makes you feel mildly, pleasantly alive, that gives you that satisfying feel of rubber pushing softly, spongily back through the shaft of a cheap pen against your moving hand.

To spend your evening writing on the sole of a slipper with a Biro (or, for that matter, writing on a banana, which offers an almost identical pleasure) is like connecting yourself through a high-speed ISDN line with the vanity of human wishes, and to acknowledge the heartbreaking, thrilling, terrifying, enjoyable absurdity of existing in the world.

I, personally, like to draw smiley faces, cartoon chickens and two-dimensional stereotypical fish. I like to quote poetry and the lyrics of the underappreciated pub-rock band Half-Man Half-Biscuit. I like to sign, extravagantly, the names of people I have never heard of. I like to use blue Biros rather than black, because the way the ink smears on the rubber looks better. But I am not prescriptive. It's your life. Knock yourself the hell out.

I say only this. This Saturday, don't go to the pub. Go to Marks & Spencer, or wherever it is that they sell those horrible slippers. Get a Biro. Return to your home. Sit in a comfy chair. Turn the slipper over, and press down. Feel the give of the rubber and the pleasurable slide of the Biro.

Sign your name. Or sign someone else's. ❖

How to Quit Smoking (for Shallow People)

By Derek Blasberg

Since kicking butts, Derek enjoys fried food, international travel and buying dead people's clothing, among other new vices

IN THE FILM Casablanca, Humphrey Bogart sits alone in a dark bar and lights up a cigarette. As the thick, grey fumes float around his handsome, brooding countenance, he sucks not only the sweet nectar of nicotine but also the alluring nonchalance that smoking has come to represent since the glamour of the silver screen. He inhales and immediately he's sophisticated, tough, complicated; we acknowledge what a rough life Bogie's had, how hard it was to send that two-timing Austrian on a plane with the Nazi-fighting revolutionary.

The association between cigs and style has been a long, successful one: Audrey Hepburn's graceful waftage in Breakfast at Tiffany's, James Dean's teenage cool in Rebel Without a Cause, Steve McQueen's scruffy and sensual toking while bare-backing a motorcycle, Bette Davis in general. Since then, cigarettes have been the go-to accessory for angst, carnal frustration, self-abuse and seduction.

> **'Self-abuse is still totally cool - hell, I would drink bleach if Brad Pitt did or snort gasoline if it made me look skinny '**

It was this promise of star quality that conceived my own half-decade love affair with those sophistication sticks: it was something to do during a conversation lull, something to look at in a club when I was waiting for something fun to happen, something to ask a good-looking fellow reveller for, the perfect way to end an indulgent meal. Cigarettes were my best friends.

But recently, the affair ended. Flipping through my beloved celebrity glossies (cf shallow), I came to a sad realisation: smoking wasn't street

Richard Morris Pushinsky

any more. Not because it's cancerous or anything (self-abuse is still totally cool – hell, I would drink bleach if Brad Pitt did, or snort gasoline if it made me skinny), but because the habit has been picked up by the wrong people. Wannabes and wanksters have replaced the sexy smokers so many of us longed to emulate, taking the pastime from rebellious to predictable.

Dean is dead, Bogart long gone; now we've got a bald-headed, baby-dropping Britney Spears, and her IQ-deficient baby-daddy Kevin Federline "rapping" about toking it big time. The poster girl for janked plastic surgery Tara Reid smokes, as does the bloated and sweaty faux-movie mogul Brandon Davis. Audrey Hepburn and Elizabeth Taylor these people are not. Their destruction of smoking cooldom caused me, in an unplanned healthy life change, to leave the wonderful world of tobacco after the pitiful recognition that I didn't look cool doing it any more. I discovered I couldn't be James Dean.

And that's how we shallow people can quit. Follow these simple directions: find a mirror in your house. Sit or stand in front of it. Light up a cig. Now look at yourself and ask: do I look like Kate Moss or do I look like a pill-popping Britney Spears? Do I look like Steve McQueen or a dumb victim waving this most gratuitous of "rebel" affectations now appropriated by those hungry for instant fame?

For me, it was the latter. Sure, some can still pull off the art of smoking – Moss falls in this category, as does Mary-Kate Olsen, who accessories her vintage tunics with packets of Marlboro Reds. But for the rest of us who fell in love with the pre-1990s glamour of the little fuckers, the moment has passed. And knowing you're uncool should be enough to make you kick the habit. Forget the patches and the creams and the pills and the hypnotist, if you think you look stupid doing it, you'll stop (Surgeon General, take note: instead of making those gross commercials, send free packets to Britney). The sad fact is that trashy hookers, fallen celebrities, portly pop stars and reality TV skanks have ruined what was a perfectly pleasant distraction.

Not to worry, though, because there are other cool ways to violate your health. Want an oral fixation that suppresses your appetite? Give bulimia a go. Want to stay in the nicotine arena? Try chewing the stuff – nothing says insouciance like spitting out stinky brown discharge. And what about snuff, which is tobacco you shove up your nose (because, sadly, you know some reality star will make cocaine uncool soon, too)? Annoyingly, it takes more than a cigarette now to be cool or rebellious. It's too common, too obvious, too easy. Oh no, if you want to be edgy now, you'll have to try harder. Like crystal meth. At least that makes you skinny. ❖

Trip out on Transcendentalism

By Victoria Gill

Victoria is a journalist and transcendental explorer whose misadventures have included being blessed by a Sufi shaykh, practising magic under ayahuasca and tracing her Folies Bergère past via regression

PICTURE YOURSELF IN a distant land, far, far away. Freed from the trivia of life, it's just you and yourself, feeling high, so high, so very, very high. In this place anything is possible – you have the power to reinvent the world you want. You'll feel and smell and hear in forms you'd never conceived possible (without being on drugs). You will take pleasure in every small thing, from the birds in the trees to a cricket on a blade to the sensation of soil beneath your feet. You'll even bag a rich partner, collect that inheritance, become a guru or (if all else fails) a healer and never, ever work for anybody else (you'll need the mornings to yourself in any case to recover from those Gaia raves and ruminate on that K seance).

> **'Transcendentalism is to float above the morass and mildew of the banal, a slave to nothing save for the pursuit of getting high'**

If you want to spend the rest of your life in a state of nirvana, then come with me and transcend. Transcendentalism is to live life on an elevated spiritual plane, floating above the morass and mildew of the banal, a slave to nothing save for the pursuit of getting high. It's religion without the doctrines: God bar the subservience, Buddhism minus the selflessness and purity and righteousness, yet flecked with unadulterated pleasure. It's spiritual ecstasy, only it's you that's the Holy Spirit, and your body a temple to sensory indulgence. Indeed, as Maharishi, the godfather of meditation (and first stop on the transcendental trail) once said: "This state of absolute bliss is the goal of all desires in life." A lifetime of miscreant

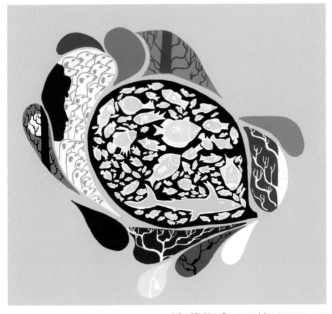

Life of Pi Alice Stevenson/alicestevenson.com

behaviour can be justified in its name.

From this day on, "*que sera*" will be your mantra, as you embrace fate and achieve a lightness of spirit that nothing can touch. Now, I want you to lie there, in stillness, swilling that notion slowly around your mind like a rich claret. Taste it. Smell it. And then, in your own time, I want you to slowly sit up. Look around you. Feel your hands. Remember the best thing that ever happened to you and how good that made you feel. And now I want you to quietly leave the room and hold that thought with you for the rest of the day.

Other people will weigh you down like an anchor given half the chance. So drop the drags. Reject the pious. Zone out when the conversation's cramping your style. If someone's really boring, say: "Can you hear that?" And they'll say: "What?" And you say: "That... Shhh." And, of course, there's nothing to hear. So you say: "Listen to the energies of the chakra." Better still, trade old friends for the brothers and sisters of the utopian 21st-century Beneficio commune in the Sierra Nevada mountains, or tune in and drop out with the Santo Daimes in Brazil, who drink ayahuasca believing it's a portal to god. Lose yourself (and your clothes) in a tantric ashram in Nepal, then seek guidance under a pure huna shaman in Maui – just don't stop. Transcendentalists are "spiritually minded" but commit to nothing. Essentially free spirits, festivals and raves are their spiritual playgrounds in their fickle, ephemeral route to the ultimate high.

There are various routes to take to elevate your soul. Find your "power animal" – the shamanistic spirit guide within you. Levitate. Do transcendental magic and get high on the insanity, glee and terror it invokes (for transcendental-lite, start off with Kabbalah). Learn to "fly", be it through yoga or sadomasochism. Set your spirit free from your body via astral projection.

Or do you want something harder? Ketamine opens the pineal gland (keeper of the third eye), opium eases you into a supremely serene "state of grace", and you didn't opt out of 2003 to trip your tits off, but were merely communing with your "plant spirit teachers" en route to the divine (think the hallucinogenic triumvirate of ayahuasca, peyote and San Pedro).

Just don't become a victim (after all, overdoses never did anybody's sense of equilibrium much good). There are legions of global SNAFUs who never make it back – from dole-loving living-room healers to opium colonies in the Sinai to hallucinogenic recluses in Central America and acid casualties in India – think Marlon Brando in Apocalypse Now, minus the cause. And if things ever do go really, really wrong, consider indulging in the mystical sphere of classical Islam by becoming a Sufi – it only takes 15 minutes to convert and the new name works wonders for throwing people off the scent of your heroin-addled past. ❖

Golf Is Life

By Dom Joly

Dom, a comedian, is not a friend
of Jimmy Tarbuck and is the
author of Letters to My Golf Club

GOLF IS PROBABLY not the first thing that springs to mind when you
decide to launch yourself into a hedonistic lifestyle – opium, the Rio
carnival and driving across America in a Ferrari with a buxom co-pilot
are probably higher on the list. Mark Twain called it "a good walk
spoiled". And yet you and Twain are wrong. To me, golf is hours of
pure, unadulterated pleasure.

I must admit that when I was younger, it really didn't appeal. The
whole "Tarbie Pro-Am" thing tarred it with a certain naffness. As I got a
bit older, however, I started to realise what it was all about – the perfect
escape. Escape from work, home, chores, family, reality, prison – take
your pick. Golf allows you almost a full day's retreat from whatever ails
you. There's the leisurely drive to the course, the four hours on the
fairways (and the rough), and a good meal and a drink or 20 afterwards
where you can lie about how well you played. Golf clears the mind of
clutter and allows you space to think, to dream and, more importantly,
to drink and smoke all you like. Great golf courses have women in little
carts driving around offering you a stocked drinks cabinet and Havana
cigars at every tee. All this in the name of sport, without cause to break
into a sweat. So a lazy bugger gets to drive a golf cart round like an
idiot, while talking complete nonsense to a good friend in beautiful
surroundings that you would never be able to create at home. What
other sport allows you these pleasures?

I've had some of my best ideas on a golf course. The medley of good
conversation and total distraction leads one to a level of clarity that is
rare in the outside world. So many ideas for TV shows, sketches,

columns etc have been born there. When I was brainstorming ideas for Trigger Happy TV, Sam Cadman (my co-conspirator and co-writer) and I sat in a Soho office for a couple of days staring at blank pieces of paper. On day three, we drove out of London and spent the next 10 days playing golf around the country at Channel 4's expense. The result was instantaneous and we returned to London full of ideas. I thought of the snail crossing the road as I hit a particularly fine shot off the third tee somewhere in Norfolk, and the idea for the squirrels came after I saw three of them hanging around in the rough like some hoodie gang on a sunny day in Inverness.

Golf is particularly useful when travelling abroad. Even the dodgiest, roughest Third World country boasts courses that command the finest geographical position. I played in Beirut during the civil war – you'd always get fine views of the sea and of the aerial bombing campaigns. Okay, so you'd have to deal with the occasional extra bunker caused by a rocket, but the entire course – like golf courses everywhere – served as a port of calm amid the storm.

I'm not a good golfer. I could be, given 30 or 40 years' practice, but it doesn't matter. The worse you are, the higher your handicap. This allows you to play someone far better and still beat them – it's very satisfying and lessens the need for anything dull, like lessons. And because the game is normally the reserve of businessmen and old fogeys, it's a delight for the younger pup. I take a particular pleasure in being the youngest by a couple of decades. There's a feeling that somehow you don't belong – it's like breaking into a millionaire's house and using his Jacuzzi, and it feels good.

It also opens up a whole new avenue of shopping for the shopaholic hedonist. Finally, you have the opportunity to seek out the famous "Golf Sale" continually advertised by bored Albanians on Oxford Street. Once in this Aladdin's cave of golf, you can dress up like Frank Sinatra, buy clubs that would be considered weapons of mass destruction by the Bush regime and remind any other half who complains about your expenditure that "it's exercise, it's good for me". Truly, whoever invented the game was a prophet. It's a form of meditation, without all the hippy bollocks. It's all about rhythm, relaxation and concentration, but while drinking, off-road driving and smoking fine cigars. That's my type of ashram, and it should be yours. ❖

How to Experience Religious Ecstasy

By Martin Deeson

Martin has heard the voice of God but insists that
he is not a schizophrenic. If he thought he was Jesus
he would know he had problems. But some days
he thinks he might once have been John the Baptist...

LONG BEFORE THERE were raves there was religious ecstasy.
Anybody reading the memoirs of ancient mystics can tell you that they
were onto a good thing. Anybody who watched Live and Let Die can
tell you the same thing about voodoo. Religious ecstasy was probably
the world's first ecstasy – apart from the act of procreation – and, of
course, they would have been immediately linked. After all, there is no
more common exclamation at the point of union than to scream: "Oh
God! I'm coming!"

Hedonism and religious ecstasy are closely related. There are many
slips twixt cup and mountaintop, but it is, after all, what most alcoholics
are looking for at the bottom of the bottle – a glimpse of the divine. It is
for this reason that amid the babble of a street drunk, one may find
pearls of wisdom worthy of the Dalai Lama (if only one can be
bothered to listen – to either of them). It's also why many of the world's
greatest mystics were, in fact, drug users, and why Indian sadhus can
attach religious significance to smoking the sacred herb.

Religious ecstasy is like a rainbow – there is little point trying to
create the right conditions for it to appear, because those conditions are
largely beyond your control. However, there are one or two things you
can do to make it more likely.

First, be born Catholic, Buddhist, Sufi Muslim or Hindu (or, in fact,
pretty much anything other than Church of England), as they are one
step closer to the top of the mountain than most other religions (with
the obvious exceptions of Rastafari and sadhus, who both have an
unfair advantage in the sheer amount of weed they smoke).

Then indulge in a little mystic tourism. As a freewheeling journalist, I have been sent on assignment to the voodoo festival of Baron Samedi in Haiti and to a gathering of 70m Hindus on the banks of the Ganges at the Kumbha Mela, and have literally heard the word of God in the Church of the Holy Sepulchre in Jerusalem. I have also had a religious experience on the Firth of Forth after a stay at the new-age Findhorn community in Scotland, so it's possible (being a heavy drinker and born Catholic) I am a little more predisposed than most.

In his wonderful essay Heaven and Hell, the philosophical mystic Aldous Huxley wrote that medieval cathedrals were designed to be psychedelic machines, with the coloured light filtering through stained-glass windows, religious music, bells and smells and the mood-changing effects of fasting for 40 days during lent – the whole thing designed to induce a religious experience on Easter Sunday. Realising the real purpose, then, behind our national landmarks of 12th-century stone, we come a little closer to appreciating one of the most powerful driving forces behind the evolution of our species, and also a little closer to the mountaintop. The urge to get out of our heads is human – the urge to get into God's head is eternal.

Alternatively, a glass of fine wine, or a good spliff and half a pill, combined with friends and a good sunset does it for me. Each to their own. But never forget, in the quest to get out of your head, you are really trying to get into the head of something bigger than yourself, so learn from the practices of the world's religions (or, for that matter, from DJs – our modern shamans who organise raves). Thus, dancing is good. Coloured lights help. Repetitive drumming is a must – or, as we now call it, house music. Drugs are essential – most religions (apart from Christianity) advocate the use of holy herbs. A good setting is conducive: it's easier to see God's face in the surface of the Ganges high on ganja than it is in the Gorbals high on smack. But at the end of the day, you can see God's face in the mirror if you're mad enough (or high enough) and some people walk around the whole time talking to God – but we tend to lock them away.

So, most of all, be open to it. Don't laugh at yourself (or do, that's the thing about this stuff, the rules are for fools) – people have been experiencing telepathy with godly matter since before humans discovered fire. Just because we now have TV and shopping malls doesn't mean we're cleverer than our ancestors. Or immune to the ultimate aim of hedonism – unity with the big raver in the sky.❖

Mississippi Michael Schmelling/michaelschmelling.com

Extreme Highs Through Extreme Sport

By Kate Spicer

Kate is a journalist, broadcaster, caner and triathlete

REMEMBER THE TOUR de France 2007 – what a bunch of caners, eh? Actually, cyclists have been popping a lot of pills since at least the 1960s. A world-class cyclist once dropped dead of a heart attack while leading the field in a race, his body fully charged with crystal meth. Sportsmen and hedonists are not, in fact, polar opposites: they are almost identical beasts. I remember chatting to an ex-pro who had given up cycling because he feared the drugs would kill him. As we chatted, he offered me an Ecstasy pill; he bit it in half and shared. And an Australian rower once told me that the Olympic village in Sydney was a hot-bed of fucking and post-race boozing. In terms of simplistic neuroscience, the sportsman and the hedonist share the same interests, actively pursuing pleasure highs to obsessive, addictive degrees.

Obviously, sportsmen are healthier as a rule. They tend not to die of lung cancer and just get a lot of muscle strains instead. The sportsman's drugs are mostly ambition and internal stimulants – thrilling neurotransmitters that drive them on and on. But other than that, they're the same. Keith Richards, Sebastian Coe – same people under the flesh. It's all about, "Fire up the dopamine receptors, and go, man, go! "

I've had my own misadventures with the drug of sport. At 35, I, the foolish, guilty hedonist, thought sport would be a form of rehabilitation. I thought it would change my behaviour. Far from saving me from excess, I got hooked on the highs of adrenalin, endorphins and numerous other excellent (and free) chemicals that the body manufactures. It started with a 10km run, then a short triathlon, then a longer one, then a double marathon, then 150 miles across the Sahara desert carrying everything on my back, then I swam to the Isle of Wight to the maddest kind of music festival – proof, if ever it were needed, that hedonism and sport go hand in hand.

This was real adventure. Training for the Sahara run, I started an affair with a former competitor, a complete K-head nutter. (His previous girlfriend had been a national-level triathlete, and a nymphomaniac not impartial to the odd line of cocaine.) As we filled ourselves with pleasure through the night, the dawn and long into the midday sun, he would say to me, like some martial-arts sensei: "Consider this part of your training. You'll survive better – you know what it is to hang on, to go without sleep. Kate. You. Are. Hardcore." I didn't believe him, but two weeks before we left for the Sahara, I went to Paris for a party, spent the night with a rapper from Atlanta and got stuck into the cocaine and pink champagne. You can imagine how bad I felt – most of my fellow endurance athletes not drinking for three months, and me, tumbling from the Eurostar into a long, dirty lunch, and then out again.

Doing sport had not, in fact, rehabilitated me into a clean-living, hard-bodied, solvent one-man woman; it merely made my body very strong. My newly potent red blood cells could deliver oxygen to my vital organs quicker, my libido shot through the roof and my party-recovery rate was better than when I was 20, especially after a race (where there is the inevitable "retoxing"). Far from keeping me out of trouble with bad boys, a lot of very strong, often young – very young indeed – men came my way. I was picking up more bad habits, not less. After the desert race, an Irish Ironman triathlete and I spent two days fucking, talking, smoking and drinking. I wore high heels throughout.

'I got hooked on the highs of adrenalin, endorphins and numerous other excellent (and free) chemicals the body manufactures'

Recently, I did a 1.5 mile competitive swim on the coast. Driving down with a triathlete, he talked me through the years when he was a nightclub promoter – he'd go straight from club to home for an hour's kip, and then do an Olympic-distance triathlon. Obviously, he vomited constantly during the race, but this has its own buzz. It's a sign you're pushing yourself enough. Vomiting's cool. He too had got into sport to tame his hedonism, he too found it severely lacking as a rehab opportunity. So he embraced their dual pleasures. Succumbed. He acquired a sad little habit – he liked to do a line of cocaine off every medal he won as soon as possible after the race, "Just to remind myself what we're doing this for." But I knew what he meant.❖

You Need Therapy

By Rose Churchill

Rose, a socialite, has spent quite a lot of time on the couch already, and when she has saved up more money, intends to return there for more

LIFE IS SO noisy these days that it is hard to be heard above the din. If nobody's ever listened to you, really listened to you – to your heart sing, to its sorrow – then therapy is the place for you. There's not a chance of reaching self-actualisation, the pinnacle of Maslow's Hierarchy of Needs, without making friends with yourself. Plus shedding the happy-go-lucky front to explore the dark side of *moi* for an hour a week can do wonders for your sex life.

> **❛In therapy, losing your sock is an emotional emergency because you say it is. And it doesn't even need to be your favourite sock❜**

The post-war generation would say, isn't listening to each other what friends are for? Gosh, no – reciprocity is such a drag. In civilised company, each person relates the banal details of their lives, and then the others get a go. If you are of relatively sound mind (and we shall assume here that you are), a spot of therapy is the equivalent of having one of those conversations and then, after a minute of tapping your foot, saying gently but firmly to your friend: "Please be quiet now. I want to talk about myself for an hour without interruption." Which is exactly what we'd all like to do anyway.

So – how best to enjoy this most nourishing of pastimes? First, do try to see it as a positive experience. You're paying, so you're in charge. Professional protocol dictates that a therapist comes to work in the morning with a neutral head on, and gives the patient unconditional, positive regard in order that the patient feels fully able to express themselves. In therapy, losing your sock is an emotional emergency

Freud Rick Morris Pushinsky

because you say it is. And it doesn't even need to be your favourite sock.

One of the best things about therapy is the two choices of seating – an armchair or a sofa. The therapist would probably prefer you to relax on a sofa because then you won't see them looking out of the window. And what could be nicer for you? Staring at the ceiling is not only gloriously restful, but also a great way of focusing the mind. It allows you to forget your therapist is there at all. The therapist is simply a trusted but faceless guide through the labyrinth of your own brilliant mind.

Do take time to tease and play with your therapist, for your own entertainment and theirs. Being as obnoxious as possible is a jolly way of testing a therapist's patience and sense of correct procedure, especially since they can't tell anybody. Don't let the people convince you that this isn't a valid aspect of therapy. Crying is just one way of releasing the drama queen that your parents never let you be. Tears are cathartic. Another bonus is that they make both patient and therapist feel like the therapy is doing something.

Watching out for signs that the therapist, despite every effort to maintain a professional reserve, is having special personal feelings for your razor-sharp wit, uncanny insight and extraordinary capacity for human empathy is one of the most rewarding aspects of therapy. Not only will they almost always let you take the credit for psychological epiphanies, but when patients are extra good, it has been known for therapists to give them the gold star of the therapy world. This is to be told that you too "could be a therapist". Unfortunately, it's rare for this not to sound like gushing.

An hour with a therapist trips along at exactly the right tempo because you are the one setting the pace. Sometimes you'll be just hitting your stride when your therapist glances discreetly at the clock on the wall and says: "I'm afraid we have to finish there." There is sadness – of course there is – because you are saying goodbye to your inner, truer self for another week. But how quickly the week passes when you're thinking about what to talk about in your next session! And soon you will be back on that sofa again, with your therapist on the edge of their seat, poised for the next exciting instalment. I know of no better way of reminding yourself that you actually exist. ❖

How to Infiltrate a Cult

By Mary Wakefield

Mary is assistant editor of The Spectator
and a natural-born believer

"THE WARS ARE not over. In fact, the worst is yet to come. But there is hope and yes, even salvation and protection, right now, offered to you by Yahweh." Yisrayl Hawkins, leader of the House of Yahweh

It's late summer and I'm standing outside the gates of a cult called the House of Yahweh. The House of Yahweh is a proper religious cult – proper like David Koresh's Branch Davidians in Waco – with a guru, groupies and guns. It's surrounded by Texan wasteland and protected by a 15ft-high fence wrapped with razor wire. But here's **step 1** of how to wheedle your way inside a community of fanatics: relax. Yes, religious extremists are paranoid and delusional, but they're not out to hurt you. The main danger of a cult is that you'll fall under its spell, not that its members will take you hostage. What use is a prisoner to people who crave disciples?

Two guards appear; they've been expecting me. They open the gates and lead me past a cluster of trailer homes up to the door of the biggest one. Two women in hijab-style headscarves stop in the pale, coarse grass and stare. I open the trailer door and come face to face with the founder and prophet Yisrayl Hawkins sitting in the gloom. He's wearing a skullcap and clicking a plastic retractable Biro, in and out, in and out. "Welcome," he says, and I thank him elaborately for agreeing to see me, because **step 2** is always show respect. You don't need an elaborate backstory or any real reason to be there if you say you're a truth-seeker. A spiritual guru believes himself to be a demi-god; he'll agree to see you and invite you to join because his hungry ego requires new converts. But never, ever talk back to him.

Hawkins talks for longer than I believe possible. The hours roll by on a tide of biblical rhetoric: the apocalypse, man's inner evil, the revelations he receives in dreams. As the light outside softens into evening orange, I'm still there saying, "Yes, absolutely, I get it," and it's true, I do. As Hawkins explains his hybrid of Judaism and Christian fundamentalism, I begin to see his appeal. He's so sure of himself and his message, it's almost tempting to believe him.

So, **step 3**, a willingness to be lightly brainwashed is essential for a cult junky. Without it, you'll be tempted to ridicule. But if even a small sneer slips from your lips, you'll be on your way home. I know this from experience. A few years ago, I trotted off to visit the Moonies in New York, hoping that they'd invite me on a training week. The Rev Chen Fong had finished his lecture on demons and was about to ask me to take part when I made a joke about Moonie mass weddings. Fong's brow furrowed. He stopped talking. My Moonie days were over, and I never got to see what makes them tick.

> **'Don't be around when cult leaders are looking for someone to blame'**

And that's the thrill of infiltrating a cult: it's not sex, drugs and rock'n'roll (though leaders do tend to grope teenage groupies), it's that moment of empathy against the odds; understanding exactly what it is that makes a man pick up poisonous snakes for the Lord, wear a pointy tin-foil hat to keep out UFO rays, or live in the desert with a chap who changed his name from Bill to Yisrayl. It's about figuring out the cocktail of narcissism and need that binds a cult together.

Step 4: know when to get out. In March 1998, I was standing in Garland, Texas, with a group of Korean men and women dressed all in white, waiting for God to descend from a spaceship onto a plywood landing platform. These people (God's Salvation Church) included academics, lawyers and psychologists, but their intelligence was no bar to outlandish belief. They'd given up everything because they thought that when God returned, it would be to a suburb of Dallas. Five, four, three, two, one… The landing time of the Lord came and went, and as incomprehension began to drift across their faces, I knew it was time to head off. The fallout from failed faith is a terrible, piteous thing and it can be incendiary. Don't be around when cult leaders are looking for someone to blame. Even if you're in quite deep, even though you'll be leaving friends behind, flee quietly and quickly without saying goodbye. Pretend you're just popping out for a snack, and never look back.❖

The Trouble with Hedonism

By Simon Munnery

Simon is a comic, the author of How to Live
and a general bad example

1. The Concise Oxford Dictionary's definition of hedonism –
"The doctrine that pleasure is the chief good or proper aim" – reminds
me of the phrase enshrined in the US Declaration of Independence:
"The right to life, liberty and the pursuit of happiness." Of course, if
you are pursuing something, by definition you haven't caught it. Why
not the right simply to be happy? Is that too much to ask? Or too little?

Is not the pursuit of happiness – this constant chasing – actually a
form of misery? "Life, liberty and the pursuit of butterflies" might be
preferable – at least butterflies can be caught. But then what? On to the
next. So it is with pleasure: if you enjoy something, you do it again, but
it's never quite as good as the first time.

2. There's no view you can't get used to and no pleasure that
doesn't fade. The road of excess may lead to the palace of wisdom,
but like all roads, it leads both ways…

3. Pleasure is a tree with many branches – sadism, the pleasure in
inflicting pain on others; masochism, the pleasure in having pain
inflicted on oneself; journalism, the pleasure in typing for cash to name
but three.

4. Pleasure is a tree with many branches, but only one trunk, the
first pleasure from which all others stem. Where does it occur?
Presumably in the womb. Surely there it's bliss; after all, babies cry
when they get out.

5. Tracing back my addictions, I wondered what was the first. Air, I realised, followed by milk – and like a fool, I mixed them. A couple of years ago, I gave up smoking and took up telling people I'd given up smoking as an alternative addiction. You get a buzz out of it. If you tell a friend, they say: "Well done!" Sometimes they even pat you on the arm. It feels good. But like a fag, it wears off after about five minutes and you've got to find another friend. Pretty soon, you're running out of friends, then it's just acquaintances. "I've given up smoking." "Who are you?" and all that. It turned out I hadn't given up smoking at all, I'd just taken up telling people I had. I was giving up between puffs. I still smoke, but I cut down and stopped for two weeks with the aid of a simple device – the harmonica. You can't have a habit vacuum – you need something to do with the hand and the mouth and the harmonica fills that gap. Suck in, blow out, instead of getting cancer get a note. Lovely, although I have discovered that harmonica players are actually less welcome than smokers in most restaurants. It's now illegal to smoke in bars – not only that, they won't let you take a drink into the tobacconists. Where's it going to end – no javelin at the opera?

6. What of the opposite of happiness – misery?

> …When the silent song you sing to yourself
> Is the only song you sing
> And your sullen face and quick quick heart
> Are the only gifts you bring
> When you find yourself at the bottom of a deep dark ditch
> Stop digging

7. Misery is a knot you tie yourself. And also a cloud that passes.

8. Time is a great healer, they say – though ultimately not, unless death be a cure.

9. The Chinese have a saying: hell is a bowl of rice – with chopsticks so long that you can't eat it. Heaven is exactly the same, but with people helping each other to eat. Such a thin line between the two.

So?

James Muldowney

10. Beware cocktails; that is, mixing your pleasures. What cannot be improved by a drink? So drink smears everything.

11. Chocolate! Coffee! Cocaine! Whatever next from South America?

12. Cocaine: waste not, want more.

13. Many drink to forget. Few forget to drink.

14. I was walking down the road the other day and I couldn't help noticing how beautiful the world was, and I thought to myself, "Why would anybody in their right mind bother to take drugs?" Then I remembered I was on drugs and that was the reason.❖

Freedom thru limertation
by billy childish

i am billy childish
ex drunk
and compulsive masturbator
late nite vomiter of good liquor
kisser of purple lipped women
riter of poems celebrating the
emptiness of my love
poems hungering for the moment
of my passion
wishing it could always be so
to never let my cock fall

Billy and Dolli (1982) Bill Hamper

When I was 21 the 17 year old Traci Emin told me that she'd been looking in a dictionary and finnaly werked out what I was. "Oh yea" I replyed "and what mite that be". "A headonist". She said "Rubish" I sneered"

Of course it was pefictly possable but I always made sure I dissagreed with Traci so as to maintain my independence, verve and superiorty. You see I was trained by my father to have a woman crying in every town, drink neat whisky by the bottle, come and go as I pleased and have a stash of hard cor-pornography as a back up. This I belived, was true freedom and it served me preety well until I was 33, then things started to fall apart. Where as I had originally counted a hero's death at aged 21, I found myself somehow still alive. My liver was shot, I suffered regular migrains which left me unable to drink smoke, eat or fuck for weeks on end – and even if I could make the ladys love me, I despised them for it because I certainly didn't love myself.

I'd had a fair innings, managing to get expeled from one of Londons better art schools; sleeping with an array of beautiful, ugly and vindictive ladys; contracting gonnareah and herpys; living a life of luxsory: 15 years on the dole, painting, riting and playing music in dubuis clubs round the world. Everything would of worked out fine if only I didn't have a body and could of lived forever.

Actually the illness saved me. Its just about acceptable to be a teenager into your mid 30's but after that, it's increasingly irratating for all concerned. So I grew myself up. It took 6 months to wean myself off the whisky, a couple of phone calls to get rid of my excess girlfriends, stopping smoking was easy because who needs fire if you haven't got water? And so I became the same friendly, free thinking little boy I'd been at aged 12. I'd always woundered how I wuold ever become a man then I realised that growing up means not having to pretend to be grown up. Along the way I underwent 7 years intense phyco therapy, got over being sexual abused as a kid; did several intensive meditation retreats; erased the last of my ambitions and stopped collecting poisionus women.

Happiness is pretty simple really, it's just being who you really are and not pretending to be interesting or having to hang around artists, pop stars, poets and other scum. 'Artists', incedently are as dull and deluded as any excutive who belives that their job, wife, or country house, defines who and what they are.

Being free is also small beer, it's not being tied to opates, alcole and our sociotys nurotic obsession with being sexy. Freedom is being free.

All in all it is boring to be a headonist in a headonistic age. Here is a manefesto against the cult of headonisim.

Freedom thru limertation

1. limitations are not obsticuls but what help make us decent and humain human beings

2. Reality, as opposed to drug indussed idocy, is what enables us to meet ourselfs and gives traction in an otherwise glutioniuss and pointless existence.

3. if you don't limit yourself nature will limit your life for you.

4. To become an adult is a fine asperation where as to be an adult despratly needing to be a teenager is pathetic.

5. That's how a country ends up with a priminster who plays the guitar, melts ice caps and conducts Orwallian wars against terrorists that can never be won. You also run the likely risk of being remembered as a compleat and utter arse.

6. It is not possible to maintain an erection forever.

7. shitting your pants, directing the traffic with a plastic bag on your head and sweating piss is not cool.

8. being cool is not cool, being cool is the new shit.

9. being alive matters and should be taken seriously.

10. Even if being alive dosnt matter it improves life behaving as if it does.

11. Every body hated Mary Whithouse but know one has the guts to admit that she was right

12. So to were the people who said that Rock 'n; roll would undermine the very fabric of socioty

13. God loves even the boring.

14. Grow up.
Headonism is rubbish becouise it is looking for god in all the rong places (drugs, booze and other peoples cunts and arses.)

A Hedonist's Guide to Death

By Sebastian Horsley

Sebastian is an artist, the author of Dandy in the Underworld
and an expert in failed suicide

Franck Allais/franckallais.com

BIRTH WAS ALMOST the death of me. When Mother found out she
was pregnant, she took an overdose. Since then, I have made dying my
life's work. I have been electrocuted, crucified and shot at. I have
overdosed with heroin, played Russian roulette and jumped out of
planes, off cliffs and into the ocean with great white sharks. I have
always wanted to have a significant death. I yearn to go out in a blaze

of glory. I'd settle for a blaze of ignominy. Yet it seems even a cheap death is hard to come by.

But it has been worth it. Life loses interest when the highest stake in the game of living – life itself – may not be risked. True excitement for man is the confrontation of death and the skilful defiance of it by watching others fed to it as he survives. Death is something that we fear, but it titillates the ear.

So, to get a taste, first try parachuting. It is a novel enough way to commit suicide. Remember, the only polite thing to do when engaged in skydiving is to die. That's what everyone is waiting around for. I only broke my leg. Here's a tip – take some drugs before you jump. I took amphetamines. It was quite interesting, speeding out of my head and speeding towards the ground like a cow wrapped in concrete.

Guns are the best method of suicide. Drugs are too chancy – you might miscalculate the dosage and just have a good time. First, ease yourself in with a game of Russian roulette. I played it once with a hooker. I picked up the gun and took out all the bullets but one. Then I spun the chamber and closed it again. I was entranced by that lovely mechanical click; the clean, cold precision, the satisfying clunk. The weight felt so right. So permanent and blank and true.

> **'I am often asked if I believe in life after death. I don't believe in life before death. Life after death is as improbable as sex after marriage'**

I raised it to my head, shut my eyes and pulled the trigger. The rush felt so brutal. It swept my brain away. I shook from the violence of my own heartbeat. Then I collapsed with that blissful, giddy, fainting sensation, lost in that heart-breaking moment of pure terror. I was speechless with happiness; choking with love.

It was an interesting experience. Coming so close to death was really like coming so close to life, because life, as it is, is nothing. I am often asked if I believe in life after death. I don't believe in life before death. Life after death is as improbable as sex after marriage.

When I die, I shall be a dead dandy atheist: someone who's all dressed up with no place to go. As long as I'm not buried alive or end up in heaven, I don't give a toss. Just put me out with the rubbish. Anything except sticking me in a goddamn cemetery, with people putting a bunch of flowers on your stomach on Sundays.

Of course I'd like to go to my own funeral. What a vast wardrobe of sartorial opportunities sorrow can provide! They say such nice things about people at their funerals that it makes me sad to realise that I'm going to miss mine by just a few days.

Death is the only thing society hasn't succeeded in completely vulgarising. It's the only thing that is truly ours. So make it yours, my darlings, as I have made it mine. I didn't die for long, but it was enough for me. I have been to the other side. And if this is dying, I don't think much of it. For the amount of publicity it gets, it's a bit of an anticlimax.

We can't really look at death any more than we can look at the sun, but we must try. We all use our personalities as trenches for the defence of our existence, as scarecrows to frighten away reality. But it is only in extreme situations that reality reveals itself. For in death, we rediscover life.

As all self-respecting dandies know, suicides are the aristocrats of death. They represent a triumph of style over life. My existence is a work of art. It deserves a frame – if only to distinguish it from the wallpaper. Suicide will look nice. It will match the home furnishings.

The only truly stylish ending to an article like this is a suicide note. Well, here is mine: "I have decided to stop living on account of the cost."

Whatever, I guess we all die in the end.

Yours temporarily, Sebastian.

Dill Pixels

The Ones That Got Away (The Ones We Turned Away)

✘ A Guide to Star Fucking

✘ A Guide to Porn Star Fucking

✘ How Not to Get into the Porn Industry

✘ How to Have Sex with Perfect Strangers

✘ How to Hit on a Foreigner Who Speaks Not a Lick of Your Language

✘ A Guide to Shagging Sheep (If That's All That's Available)

✘ How and Why to Marry a Gay Man

✘ The Mortal Sin of Masturbation

✘ How to Drink Booze for Breakfast and Avoid the 12-Step Programme

✘ How to Take Heroin and Not Become a Junkie

✘ How to Surf on LSD

✘ How to Con a Granny Out of Her Savings

✘ How to Have a Perfectly Nice Day at the Beach While Engaging in Seriously Dangerous and Highly Illegal Political Activism

✘ The Joy of a Good Shit

✘ How and Why to Have a Nervous Breakdown

✘ A Guide to Leisure Satanism

✘ How to Get High on Voodoo

✘ The Lure of Self Destruction

Editor's note: things could have been a lot worse, see.

Acknowledgments

What you hold in your hands is nothing short of a small miracle. That's less a deluded boast, more a tribute to the improbability of 50-odd pro-pleasure-seekers downing toys, declining invites and staying in to do their homework. So, first, thank you to each and every contributor, for all their extraordinarily excellent essays, however late they were.

Then, repeat thanks to particular writers for their special consultative services: Alex Needham, Bethan Cole, Lucas Hollweg, Simon Mills, Kate Spicer, Tom Stubbs and Mary Wakefield. Thanks, too, for the suggestions, counsel and friendly shoulders from Sophie Biggs, Abid David, Jessie Brinton, Sally-Anne Limb, Jeanine Pepler, Chloe Stirling, Adam Thompson, Spoon Newell, Miki Watson, Gemma Soames and Ollie Wright.

Thank you, too, to Jason Morris, this book's most able designer, for creating such a handsome object that any bookshelf would look all the better for, and also for his open-all-hours advice bureau. Thank you to Janine Thomas, a mistake-catcher of the highest order. And to Tremayne Carew Pole, the dark master himself of the A Hedonist's Guide to…. series, for this was all his idea.

And finally, thank you to my friends and family, for their cheerleading dances and rallying cries, for parachuting in provisions, and for invitations to breakouts for the purposes of "fieldwork". And, of course, to mister miraculous himself, Miko Vranic.

A Hedonist's Manifesto by Fleur Britten © Fleur Britten; For the Love of Lunch by Joseph Connolly © Joseph Connolly; A Table for One by Dom Joly © Dom Joly; How to Seduce… with Champagne by Lucas Hollweg © Lucas Hollweg; Eat Lobster in a War Zone by Martin Deeson © Martin Deeson; The Wisdom and Folly of Whisky by Joseph Connolly © Joseph Connolly; A Cigar Is Just a Cigar by Reg Gadney © Reg Gadney; I Love Hangovers by Simon Munnery © Simon Munnery; How to Be an Absolute Disgrace by David Piper © David Piper; The Heavenly Virtues of Outrageous Hosts by Fleur Britten © Fleur Britten; Nonstop Hedonism by Tiffanie Darke © Tiffanie Darke; Party SOS: How to Rescue a Shite Night by Fleur Britten © Fleur Britten; Dance Like Everyone's Watching by Tom Stubbs © Tom Stubbs; Rule Like a Drag Queen by Jodie Harsh © Jodie Harsh; How to Be a Hedonist Until You Die by Kate Spicer © Kate Spicer; A Hedonist's Record Collection by Alex Needham © Alex Needham; The DJing Game by Tabitha Denholm © Tabitha Denholm; Your Life Will Be Better if You Play Guitar by Will Hodgkinson © Will Hodgkinson; How to Survive Festivals Without Really Trying by Bill Brewster © Bill Brewster; Caned and Able - a Sensible Guide to Gear by Howard Marks © Howard Marks; Cook with Cannabis Without OD-ing Your Guests by Tim Pilcher © Tim Pilcher; How to Score Drugs Abroad (and I Don't Mean Ibiza) by Martin Deeson © Martin Deeson; A Field Guide to Magic Mushrooms by Patrick Harding © Patrick Harding; An Homage to Pillage by James Delingpole © James Delingpole; Psychoactivity in the Strangest Places by Howard Marks © Howard Marks; Life Through the K Hole by Charlie Norton © Charlie Norton; Drugs – A Doctor's Honest View by Dr Chloe Britten © Dr Chloe Britten; First Base: On the Pull by Tom Stubbs © Tom Stubbs; How to Visit a Lap Dancing Club (Without Losing All Your Money or Self-Respect) by Martin Deeson © Martin Deeson; The Craft of the Cad by David Piper © David Piper; A Cock Is for Teasing by Catherine Townsend © Catherine Townsend; The Straight Man's Guide to Cruising by Paul Flynn © Paul Flynn; The Rough Guide to Sex by Rebecca Newman © Rebecca Newman; Sex Party Etiquette by Catherine Townsend © Catherine Townsend; How to Handle a Hooker by Sebastian Horsley © Sebastian Horsley; Less Is Never More by Camilla Morton © Camilla Morton; Get Ahead in the Art World by Nick Hackworth © Nick Hackworth; Join the Jet Set by Oscar Humphries © Oscar Humphries; How to Be a Star by Andrew Stone © Andrew Stone; The Ten Commandments of Surf God-Dom by Jamie Brisick © Jamie Brisick; What You Can Really Get out of Concierge by Imogen Edwards-Jones © Imogen Edwards-Jones; Live Like a High Roller on a Lowlife Budget by Simon Mills © Simon Mills; Wing it with Jets, Boats and Hookers by Oscar Humphries © Oscar Humphries; A Hedonist's Guide to Decadent Travel by Nick Bornoff © Nick Bornoff; How to Pick a Horse in a Paddock by Sir Clement Freud © Sir Clement Freud; Poker Skills for Life by Eliza Burnett © Eliza Burnett; Gambling Is Good for You by Michael Holden © Michael Holden; Hedonism in the Home by Jenny Éclair © Jenny Éclair; The Cucumber's Guide to Cool by Tom Stubbs © Tom Stubbs; How to Gatecrash by Nicholas Allan © Nicholas Allan; Breaking the Law for a Laugh by Martin Deeson © Martin Deeson; Freeloaders Will Save the World by Fleur Britten © Fleur Britten; Skive for a Salary by Tom Hodgkinson © Tom Hodgkinson; In Praise of Protests by Dan Kieran © Dan Kieran; Blag Your Way Backstage by Moby © Moby; How to Be a Rock'n'roll Rebel by Miranda Sawyer © Miranda Sawyer; Sweet Talk the Cops by Tom Stubbs © Tom Stubbs; A Hedonist's Guide to Prison Survival by Howard Marks © Howard Marks; A Teetotaller's Guide to Hedonism by Will Storr © Will Storr; The Thrills of Guerrilla Gardening by Richard Reynolds © Richard Reynolds; Get out of Your Head on Yoga by Tony Marcus © Tony Marcus; The Selfish Benefits of Random Acts of Kindness by Cynthia Parsons McDaniel © Cynthia Parsons McDaniel; Another Countryside by Bethan Cole © Bethan Cole; Ten Steps to Freedom by Tom Hodgkinson © Tom Hodgkinson; Cycling in the City by Mary Wakefield © Mary Wakefield; The Point of Pointlessness by Sam Leith © Sam Leith; How to Quit Smoking (for Shallow People) by Derek Blasberg © Derek Blasberg; Trip out on Transcendentalism by Victoria Gill © Victoria Gill; Golf Is Life by Dom Joly © Dom Joly; How to Experience Religious Ecstasy by Martin Deeson © Martin Deeson; Extreme Highs Through Extreme Sport by Kate Spicer © Kate Spicer; You Need Therapy by Rose Churchill © Rose Churchill; How to Infiltrate a Cult by Mary Wakefield © Mary Wakefield; The Trouble with Hedonism by Simon Munnery © Simon Munnery; Freedom Through Limitation by Billy Childish © Billy Childish; The Hedonist's Guide to Death by Sebastian Horsley © Sebastian Horsley.